Birnbaum's

Walt Disney World

for KIDS

by kids

THE OFFICIAL GUIDE

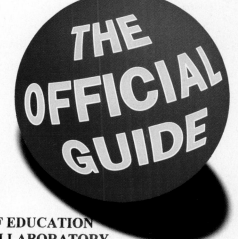

Jill Safro
Editor

Deanna Caron
Managing Editor

Todd Sebastian Williams
Art Director

Elisa Gallaro
Senior Editor

Suzy Goytizolo
Assistant Editor

Alexandra Mayes Birnbaum
Consulting Editor

HYPERION AND HEARST BUSINESS PUBLISHING, INC.

ISBN: 0-7868-8369-3

Printed in the United States of America

An enormous debt of gratitude is owed to Regina Maher, Carter Schultz,
Laura Simpson, Julie Woodward, Kevin Banks, Gene Duncan, Tim Lewis, Wendy Meere,
Alicia Laing, John Fischer, Elaine K. Cavanaugh, Greg Otte, Tammi Jacob, Tom Hoof,
Reggie White, Aavo Harju, Pamela Reuter, Loraine Pimentel, and LuAnn Newcomer, all
of whom performed above and beyond the call of duty to make the creation of this book
possible. To Phil Lengyel, Tom Elrod, Linda Warren, Bob Miller, and Charlie Ridgway,
thank you for believing in this project in the first place. And to Wendy Lefkon, special
thanks for taking it from idea to reality.

We'd also like to tip our hats to Tom Passavant, editorial director, and to Louise Collazo,
copy editor extraordinaire.

Other 1999 Birnbaum's Official Disney Guides

Disneyland
Walt Disney World
Walt Disney World Without Kids

CONTENTS

When you first got the news, you couldn't believe your own ears. Could it be true? Were you really going on a vacation to Walt Disney World? Well, believe it or not, it's true! Before you know it, you'll be in the sunny state of Florida. It's the home of Walt Disney World and the most famous mouse on planet Earth. (Hint: His name starts with "M.")

   If you have ever been there, you already know that it's one mighty big place. It has theme parks, water parks, pools, petting zoos, and more. Everywhere you turn there is something exciting to see or do. In fact, there is so much going on that it can get a little confusing. That's where this book comes in handy. It describes everything in the World, from the

Disney World!

Magic Kingdom theme park to the Hoop-Dee-Doo Musical Review. And it's filled with hot tips and advice from kids like you.

There is no right or wrong way to read this book. You can start on the first page and read straight through to the end. Or you can skip around, read your favorite parts first, and come back to the rest later.

No matter what you do, one thing is for sure: When you're done, you will be a true-blue Disney expert. Soon kids may start asking *you* for advice on how to have the most awesome vacation in the World!

PACK A PENCIL

Don't leave this book behind when you head for the parks. Reading it is a good way to pass the time while waiting in line for Splash Mountain or The Haunted Mansion. There are games and activities inside, too (you'll need a pen or colored pencils for some of them). Here are a few other ways to use the book while visiting the wonderful world of Disney:

● Put a check mark next to an attraction once you've seen it. That way you'll know what's left to see on your next trip.

● Give each attraction a grade. If you love it, give it an A. If you'd rather go to the dentist than sit through it again, give it a great big F. Anything in-between gets a B, C, or D.

● Ask Disney characters to autograph this book. (There is a place for autographs on page 111.)

These are the big kids who had a great time helping to put this book together (from left to right: Todd, Mickey, Jill, and Deanna).

Disney Words

What do YOU think?

Do you agree or disagree with any of the kids in this book? Let us know. Keep track of your thoughts in a diary about your Walt Disney World trip. When you get back, send your opinions and "hot tips" in a letter to the editors at:

Walt Disney World For Kids, By Kids 1999
1790 Broadway, 6th Floor
New York, NY 10019

They will read every letter before they work on next year's book.

Audio-Animatronics: Life-like robots, from birds and dinosaurs to movie stars and presidents. They seem real—but they're not.

Cast Member: A Disney employee.

Circle-Vision 360: A movie that surrounds you. The screens form a circle.

Guidemap: A theme park map that also describes attractions, shops, restaurants, and entertainment.

Imagineer: A creative person who designs Disney theme park attractions.

Meet the Experts

Kirsti and Amy (back, left to right), Seth and Robbie (front, left to right) had a blast working on this book!

It's a lot of fun to work on a book like *Walt Disney World For Kids, By Kids*. But it's also a lot of hard work. Every year, a group of kids goes to Walt Disney World with the editors of *Birnbaum's Walt Disney World*. They spend days riding attractions, splashing in pools, and chomping on delicious munchies. (That's

Kirsti Harju
Kirsti lives in Somerset, New Jersey. She was 9 years old when she worked on this book. Kirsti loves kickball, basketball, and bike riding. She also likes to cook and play the violin. Kirsti has two cats and a fish.

Seth Reuter
Seth lives in Boca Raton, Florida. He was 10 years old when he worked on this book. He spends his free time doing karate and learning about paleontology. When Seth grows up, he wants to work for NASA.

Robbie Pimentel
Robbie lives in Richmond, New York. He was 10 years old when he worked on this book. Robbie enjoys playing hockey and video games. He is also interested in computers and has his own Web site.

Amy Newcomer
Amy lives in Paupack, Pennsylvania. She was 13 years old when she worked on this book. Shopping is one of Amy's favorite things to do. She also loves skiing and playing field hockey.

the fun part.) At the end of each day, the kids have a meeting to talk about their adventures. (That's the work part.) They talk about everything they did and saw. What's cool? What's not? Who chickened out at Space Mountain? The kids also keep journals about their Disney experiences. This book could not have been written without them.

A new group of kids works on this book each year. Who are these kids and where do they come from? You can read about them above and in the pages that follow. The information will give you an idea of whose opinions might be like your own. Their words—along with other descriptions in the book—may help you decide which attractions you just have to see and which you'd like to skip.

HAVE A GREAT TRIP!

Justin Berfield, 1995

Justin lives in Oak Park, California. He was 8 years old when he worked on this book. Justin is an actor, and has been in many movies. He loves animals and has some unusual pets.

Robert Raack, 1994

Robert lives in Eugene, Oregon. He was 8 years old when he worked on this book. Robert is very interested in dragons. He likes to play video games and soccer.

Szasha Ozard, 1998

Szasha (pronounced SAH-sha) lives in Petrolia, California. She was 8 years old when she worked on this book. Szasha likes bike riding, fishing, and hiking. She also enjoys making puppets and sewing.

Lindsay Compton, 1995 & '96

Lindsay lives in Dallas, Texas. She was 9 the first year she worked on this book. She is a Girl Scout and also likes to play soccer and basketball. Lindsay loves to draw and wants to be an animal doctor someday.

Emma Peters-Axtell, 1997

Emma lives in Duluth, Minnesota. She was 9 years old when she worked on this book. Emma was on the editorial board of the *New Moon* magazine published in her hometown. She also likes to sing and dance.

Taran Noah Smith, 1994

Taran was 9 years old when he worked on this book. He plays Mark Taylor on the show "Home Improvement." When he's not on the set, he lives in San Rafael, California. He likes to sail and ride his mountain bike.

Bradley Sanchez, 1995

Bradley lives in Independence, Missouri. He was 10 years old when he worked on this book. Bradley likes to play football and is a fan of the Kansas City Chiefs. He enjoys playing video games.

Brian Foster, 1997

Brian lives in Woodinville, Washington. He was 10 years old when he worked on this book. Brian enjoys all kinds of sports and likes to work on computers. He also collects coins and rocks.

Dan Marchand, 1998

Dan lives in Clifton Park, New York. He was 10 years old when he worked on this book. His favorite hobbies are playing video games and all kinds of sports. Dan also likes to play the viola.

Michael Howard, 1998

Michael lives in San Antonio, Texas. He was 11 years old when he worked on this book. Michael enjoys playing basketball and football. He also loves to draw. Michael has two sisters.

Ashley Pletz, 1994

Ashley lives in Chicago, Illinois. She was 11 years old when she worked on this book. Ashley really loves to write. She also takes ballet lessons and has done some modeling.

Danielle Gould, 1995

Danielle lives in Potomac, Maryland. She was 11 years old when she worked on this book. Danielle enjoys reading and loves to dance. She takes ballet, jazz, and tap lessons.

Dawna Boone, 1995 & '96
Dawna lives in Natick, Massachusetts. She was 11 the first year she worked on this book. She loves to read and listen to music. She also enjoys playing the saxophone.

Lissy Woodhams, 1994
Lissy lives in Tucson, Arizona. She was 11 years old when she worked on this book. She plays the piano, is a member of a drama club, and enjoys horseback riding and going swimming.

Brian Levinthal, 1994
Brian lives in Huntington, New York. He was 12 years old when he worked on this book. He is studying cartoon art, and plays the clarinet in his school band. He also likes to swim.

Ashley Johnson, 1997
Ashley lives in Burbank, California. She was 12 years old when she worked on this book. Ashley is an actress who has been on many television shows, including "Growing Pains." She has nine pets.

Adam Farkas, 1997
Adam lives in Miami Beach, Florida. He was 12 years old when he worked on this book. His favorite sports are hockey and football. Adam also enjoys hiking, rock climbing, and waterskiing.

Danielle Thomas, 1998
Danielle lives in Danville, Kentucky. She was 12 years old when she worked on this book. Danielle enjoys church activities and going to school. She also plays the saxophone and does gymnastics.

Anna Kerlek, 1995
Anna lives in Chagrin Falls, Ohio. She was 13 years old when she worked on this book. Anna is on her school volleyball, basketball, and track teams, and she loves to sing and play the piano.

Tate Lynche, 1995 & '96
Tate was 13 the first year he worked on this book, and was a Mouseketeer on the "Mickey Mouse Club" show. He lives in St. Petersburg, Florida. Tate also enjoys in-line skating.

David Bickel, 1994
David lives in Columbus, Ohio. He was 13 years old when he worked on this book. David is a sports fan and enjoys playing baseball and video games. His favorite teams are the Atlanta Braves and the Chicago Bulls.

Karyn Williams, 1994 & '96
Karyn lives in Orlando, Florida. She was 13 the first year she worked on this book. Karen is an aspiring actress. She also loves to travel, and once spent several weeks studying marine biology in Australia.

Adam Winchester, 1995
Adam was 14 years old when he worked on this book. He lives in Colorado Springs, Colorado. He loves hockey, basketball, baseball, and soccer. He hopes to become an architect or to work with computers.

Nita Booth, 1994
Nita lives in Chesapeake, Virginia. She was 14 years old when she worked on this book. Nita was a Mouseketeer on the "Mickey Mouse Club" show. She loves to sing and is a member of her church choir.

Meet Walt Disney

When Walt Disney was a little boy he would look up at the sky and imagine the clouds were animals. As the wind pushed a cloud, a pig would turn into a cow. Soon, the cow would become a chicken! It was then Walt realized that anything could become a reality with a little imagination.

But he knew that success wouldn't come from daydreaming alone. Growing up on a farm had taught him the importance of hard work. And it's a good thing, because without Walt's hard work we would never have met the most famous mouse in the world.

A mouse is born

In 1928, Walt created a little cartoon mouse (who he almost named Mortimer. Luckily, Lilly Disney convinced her husband to name him Mickey!). Mickey Mouse was an instant success. But one hit wasn't enough for his creator. Walt was always looking for new challenges. In 1937, his animation company made the first full-length cartoon movie: *Snow White and the Seven Dwarfs*. Walt was very proud that he had made a movie for everyone in the family to enjoy.

Family was very important to Walt. Every Sunday, he would do something special with his two daughters. They often went to amusement parks. The kids loved it, but Walt was sad that there weren't rides for parents. "I wish there were a place that children *and* grown-ups could have fun," he thought.

A dream is a wish your heart makes

Since a place like that didn't exist, Walt decided to build it. At first he was going to call it Mickey Mouse Park, but then he named it Disneyland. It was so popular that Walt's new dream was to build an even bigger park: Disney World. He must have wished upon a star—because his dream came true.

 # WHERE'S MICKEY?

Did you know that Mickey Mouse just celebrated his 70th birthday? That's a lot of candles for a mouse to blow out! Mickey made his debut in 1928, in a movie called *Steamboat Willie*. Back then, he was drawn in black and white. He certainly has changed over the years!

Even so, Mickey is usually easy to spot—especially at Walt Disney World. He marches in parades, dances in shows, and greets guests in the theme parks. But it can sometimes be tough to find him. Why? He's hidden! There are "Hidden Mickey" images all over Walt Disney World. (Many look like the three connected circles that form Mickey's head.) You might see them in shadows, lights, drawings, or even in the clouds at some attractions. How many can you find? Mickey's garden in Toontown Fair is a great place to start your search. Happy hunting!

What a Wonderful World

Walt Disney loved dreaming up stories to tell and new ways to tell them. After he died, his brother, Roy, kept one of his biggest dreams alive. He made sure Walt's special "world" was built just the way he had imagined it. Roy even insisted that it be called *Walt Disney World*, so everyone would know it was his brother's dream.

Walt Disney World officially opened on October 1, 1971. Since then, millions of people have stopped in for a visit. Some people come to Walt Disney World for a day, but most stay a little longer. There's just so much to see and do.

Pick a theme park, any theme park

The most famous part of Walt Disney World is the **Magic Kingdom**. It's home to Cinderella Castle, Space Mountain, and those rascally Pirates of the Caribbean. It's also where Mickey, Minnie, and their pals keep their country cottages. Kids of all ages can't get enough of this happy place. Of course, there are three other theme parks to see.

Epcot is a wonderland of science and discovery. It's also a great place to take a "world tour." Eleven different countries have shops, restaurants, and attractions inside the theme park. Epcot opened in 1982. You weren't even born yet!

Are you a major movie fan? If so, you'll get a big kick out of the **Disney-MGM Studios** theme park. It's jam-packed with movie-themed rides and exhibits. The secrets of animation are revealed at The Magic of Disney Animation.

Belle and Gaston sing their hearts out at Beauty and the Beast Live on Stage. And The Twilight Zone Tower of Terror scares *everybody* silly. The Disney-MGM Studios opened in 1989. How old were you then?

Disney's Animal Kingdom is the newest theme park at Walt Disney World. (It got off to a *roaring* start in 1998.) It has what it takes to make any kid's day: an African safari ride filled with wild animals, life-like dinosaurs, and a super slimy 3-D movie about bugs.

Chill out!

Need to cool off on a hot day? You can make a splash at a Disney water park. Between **River Country**, **Typhoon Lagoon**, and **Blizzard Beach**, it's almost impossible to stay dry. Each one has slippery slides, tube rides, and some very cool pools.

But wait—there's more! Walt Disney World also has boats, bikes, and even horses to ride. It has hundreds of restaurants, shops, and other places to explore. In fact, no matter how many times you visit, there's always something new to see. Will Walt Disney World ever be finished? Not as long as there is imagination left in the world. That's exactly how Walt would have wanted it.

Planning a vacation to Walt Disney World is lots of fun. But it's not as easy as it sounds. There are so many choices to make! Which parks should you visit? What should you pack? And where can you meet your favorite Disney characters? Use this book to answer these questions and help plan your family's vacation. Remember: It's never too early to get started!

Disney World

Save Room for Souvenirs

When you pack for your trip, make sure you're prepared for the weather. Believe it or not, it gets chilly in Florida, especially in the winter. But during the summer it's sizzling hot! It's usually warm during the rest of the year. Layers are a good idea, so you can take something off if you get hot. Remember to pack clothes and shoes that are lightweight and comfortable—since you'll do a lot of walking at the parks. And don't overstuff your suitcase. You'll need room for all the goodies you buy at Walt Disney World.

What else should you bring? That's up to you! Here's a short list to help you get started:

- **A sweatshirt or sweater**
- **Broken-in sneakers or shoes**
- **Shorts and pants**
- **Long-sleeved and short-sleeved shirts**
- **A bathing suit**
- **Sunscreen**
- **A hat**

Visit Disney on the Internet

This book is chock-full of information about Disney, but there is another great place to learn about Walt Disney World: the Internet. Visit Disney's Web site at *www.disneyworld.com*.

It has maps to download, and new pictures and stories every day. If you have a question, send an e-mail message and you will get an answer in a few days. If you have a question and don't have access to the Internet, write to Walt Disney World at:

Walt Disney World
Box 10000
Lake Buena Vista, FL 32830

15

Ten Days Till

10 DAYS

SING "ZIP-A-DEE-DOO-DAH"
—THE FINAL COUNTDOWN TO YOUR TRIP HAS BEGUN!

9

MAKE YOUR OWN MOUSE EARS

Tape strips of paper together to make a loop big enough to fit around your head. Then cut out two circles and tape them to the front of the loop. It's easy!

6

LESS THAN A WEEK TO GO!
Celebrate by coloring in the Cheshire Cat.

5 MORE DAYS

This is a picture of:
(a) Spaceship Earth (b) Space Mountain
(c) a giant golf ball

2 DAYS TO GO!

This carnotaurus is in Disney's Animal Kingdom. You can visit it at:
(a) Camp Minnie-Mickey (b) Countdown to Extinction (c) It's a Small World

1 DAY LEFT

Get a good night's sleep—tomorrow is a big day! (Don't forget to pack your toothbrush.)

ANSWERS: **[8]** Magic Kingdom; **[5]** Spaceship Earth; **[3]** the park turns 10 this year; **[2]** Countdown to Extinction

Disney!

7
IT'S PARTY TIME!
Work with your parents to plan a Mickey party or a Disney dinner. Don't forget to wear your mouse ears.

8 DAYS LEFT
When Walt Disney World opened in 1971, it had just one theme park. Do you know which one it was?

3

The Disney-MGM Studios theme park opened on May 1, 1989. How old does that make it?

4
TIME TO PACK

Today's the day:

MONTH/DAY/YEAR

You're going to Walt Disney World!

Magic Kingdom

When most people hear the words Walt Disney World, they think of Cinderella Castle, Space Mountain, and, of course, Mickey Mouse. They are all here in the Magic Kingdom, along with much more. That's why so many kids say the Magic Kingdom is the most special part of the World.

You can spend lots of time in its seven lands—Main Street, U.S.A., Adventureland, Frontierland, Liberty Square, Fantasyland, Mickey's Toontown Fair, and Tomorrowland. This chapter can help you decide which attractions you want to see first. Then make a list of your second choices and a list of the things you can save for another visit. That way you can organize your visit and avoid wasting precious time.

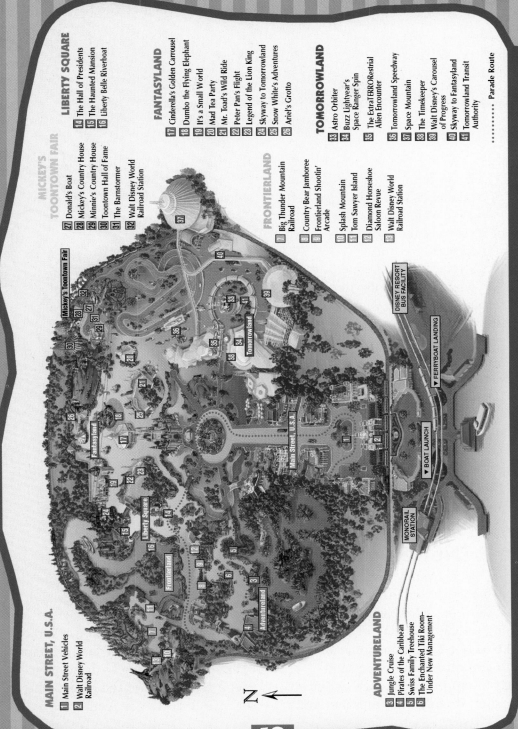

MAIN STREET, U.S.A.

1 Main Street Vehicles
2 Walt Disney World Railroad

MICKEY'S TOONTOWN FAIR

27 Donald's Boat
28 Mickey's Country House
29 Minnie's Country House
30 Toontown Hall of Fame
31 The Barnstormer
32 Walt Disney World Railroad Station

LIBERTY SQUARE

14 The Hall of Presidents
15 The Haunted Mansion
16 Liberty Belle Riverboat

FANTASYLAND

17 Cinderella's Golden Carousel
18 Dumbo the Flying Elephant
19 It's a Small World
20 Mad Tea Party
21 Mr. Toad's Wild Ride
22 Peter Pan's Flight
23 Legend of the Lion King
24 Skyway to Tomorrowland
25 Snow White's Adventures
26 Ariel's Grotto

FRONTIERLAND

7 Big Thunder Mountain Railroad
8 Country Bear Jamboree
9 Frontierland Shootin' Arcade
10 Splash Mountain
11 Tom Sawyer Island
12 Diamond Horseshoe Saloon Revue
13 Walt Disney World Railroad Station

TOMORROWLAND

33 Astro Orbiter
34 Buzz Lightyear's Space Ranger Spin
35 The ExtraTERRORestrial Alien Encounter
36 Tomorrowland Speedway
37 Space Mountain
38 The Timekeeper
39 Walt Disney's Carousel of Progress
40 Skyway to Fantasyland
41 Tomorrowland Transit Authority

········· Parade Route

ADVENTURELAND

3 Jungle Cruise
4 Pirates of the Caribbean
5 Swiss Family Treehouse
6 The Enchanted Tiki Room—Under New Management

This is a map of the Magic Kingdom. You can get a bigger one at the park. They're free!

19

Main Street, U.S.A.

Are you ready for some time traveling? You'll do a lot of it in the Magic Kingdom. Four out of its seven lands send you either back or forward in time.

Main Street, U.S.A., is one of those lands. It was made to look like a small American town in the year 1900. (Some of it is based on the town Walt Disney grew up in—Marceline, Missouri.)

There are pretty lampposts, horse-drawn trolleys, and many other touches that make the street charming. If you look both ways before crossing, you'll notice a big difference between this Main Street and a real one: There's a castle at the end of it!

There are no major rides or attractions here, but Main Street, U.S.A, is still a fun place to be. You can sink your teeth into fresh-baked cookies, hop aboard a train, or sit on the curb and watch a parade go by.

Walt Disney World Railroad

Walt Disney loved trains. He even had a miniature one in his backyard that was big enough to ride on.

The Magic Kingdom trains are real locomotives that were built nearly a hundred years ago. A full trip takes about 20 minutes, but you can get on or off at any station (at Main Street, U.S.A., Frontierland, or Mickey's Toontown Fair).

What do the kids who worked on this book think about the railroad? They love traveling by train. You get a great view of the park—plus a chance to rest your feet.

Main Street Vehicles

The railroad isn't the only transportation on Main Street, U.S.A. Horse-drawn trolleys, old-fashioned cars, and an antique fire engine make trips up and down the street throughout the day.

You can climb aboard any one of these vehicles in Town Square or by Cinderella Castle. Each trip is strictly one-way—you'll be asked to hop off after the ride.

The vehicles don't operate every day. Stop by City Hall (it's on Main Street) to find out when they run.

When it isn't chugging along the street, the fire engine is on display at the Main Street firehouse. Feel free to stop in and take a peek.

Adventureland

A trip to Adventureland is like a visit to a tropical island. It has so many plants and trees that George of the Jungle would feel right at home. (Don't bother looking for him. He prefers his own treehouse to the one here. Besides, he probably couldn't find it if he tried.)

As you can tell from the name of this land, the attractions take you on exciting (and silly) adventures.

Jungle Cruise

It's a good thing elephants aren't shy. Otherwise, they might get upset when you watch them take a bath. That's just one of the interesting sights on the Jungle Cruise.

The voyage goes through the jungles of Africa and Asia. Along the way you see life-like zebras, giraffes, lions, hippos, and a few headhunters. (Don't worry—the only real animals in the ride are the humans inside the boat!)

If you love silly jokes, you'll definitely love this ride. The captain tells a bunch of them.

Some kids wish the ride were more exciting. "I love the ride," says Robert. "But it would be even cooler if the headhunters threw their spears."

The Jungle Cruise is usually very crowded—try to get there early in the morning. It's best to ride during the day, when you can see everything.

"This is a really good ride for anyone at any age." Amy (age 13)

Pirates of the Caribbean

Ahoy, there, maties! There's rough waters ahead! That's the warning a pirate gives near the start of this attraction. He must be a wimpy pirate, because kids don't think this ride is rough at all. (But there is a small dip and some dark scenes, so be prepared.)

The journey takes place in a little boat. After floating through a quiet cave . . . *BOOM!* You're in the middle of a pirate attack! Cannons blast while the song "Yo Ho, Yo Ho; a Pirate's Life for Me" plays over and over again. Watch for a pirate with his leg hanging over a bridge—the leg is really hairy.

Most kids give the pirates a thumbs-up. "This is a really good ride for anyone at any age," says Amy. Szasha says, "It's slow, but that's so you can look at the scenery around you." Dan would like more action. "When I was younger it was my favorite ride. But now I think there should be more drops," he says.

> **❝Once you know the story, the treehouse is fascinating.❞**
>
> **David (age 13)**

Swiss Family Treehouse

What would it be like for your family to be stranded on an island? John Wyss asked his kids this question before he wrote a book called *The Swiss Family Robinson*. Together they came up with lots of crazy adventures for the Robinsons. They survive a shipwreck, fight off pirates, and build the most awesome treehouse in the world.

Just like the movie

Walt Disney Productions made a movie based on the book in 1960. The Swiss Family Treehouse in Adventureland looks just like the treehouse in the film. In it, you climb a staircase to many different levels. Each room has lots to see. The tree itself looks very real, but it's not. It has 300,000 plastic leaves, and concrete roots.

An excellent story

Everyone agrees that reading the story or seeing the movie *Swiss Family Robinson* makes the treehouse more fun to explore. "Once you know the story, the treehouse is fascinating," says David. "I like the boys' room with the hammocks and the running water."

Robert knows the story, so he understood what he was seeing. "I could name all the rooms as we walked around," he says. "It's an excellent treehouse."

HOT TIP!

Even if you have been here before, go again. It's a whole new show.

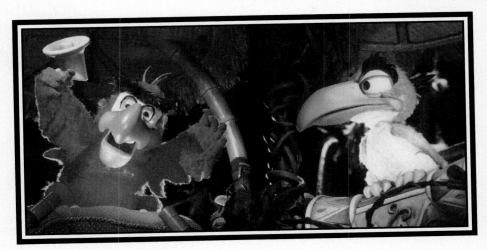

The Enchanted Tiki Room— Under New Management

Birds rule at this attraction. They also sing and crack lots of jokes. If you've been here before, you may know José, Michael, Fritz, and Pierre. They've been singing old favorites, like "The Tiki, Tiki, Tiki Room," for more than 25 years.

Now the Tikis are "Under New Management." They have a new show and new bosses. One is Iago, who's as loud and cranky as he was in *Aladdin*. The other is the very nervous Zazu from *The Lion King*. Thanks to Iago, Zazu has plenty to worry about in the Tiki Room.

It seems Iago hasn't just joined the show—he has taken over! Zazu warns that changes might make the Tiki gods angry. But Iago just laughs.

Suddenly, the Tiki goddess of disaster appears. Her name is Uh Oa, and she is very angry. Zap! She shows Iago who's really boss—and makes him disappear.

Now it's the Tiki gods' turn to prove that they can sing as well as the birdies sing. Iago is allowed back to see the gods perform a hip-hop song—and he becomes their biggest fan.

Frontierland

Howdy, pardners! And welcome to the wild west. Frontierland shows you what America was like when pioneers first settled west of the Mississippi River. It's also where you'll find two of the best rides in the Magic Kingdom. Both of them are special Disney mountains. You can take a watery trip down Splash Mountain and ride a runaway train at Big Thunder Mountain Railroad. These are just a few of the fun things to do here.

Splash Mountain

After riding Splash Mountain, you'll know how it got its name. It's impossible to stay dry! There are three small dips, leading up to a giant, watery drop.

You're all wet

Brad loves getting wet. That's why he likes to sit up front when he rides Splash Mountain. "When you're in the front, you get all drenched," he says. You don't get as soaked in the back, but "you feel airborne," Kirsti says.

The scenery tells a story

The kids agree that you have to go on it a few times before you can understand the ride's story. (You travel through scenes from Walt Disney's movie *Song of the South*.) Lindsay says, "Every time there's a little splash, something different happens to Brer Rabbit." Brad says, "Brer Rabbit is supposed to be in the log getting away from the fox and the bear." When the rabbit goes over the edge toward

the end, you go along for the ride. (Try to keep your eyes open during the big drop—it won't be easy.)

Tate thinks that following the story "makes the ride even better." Karyn agrees. "All the characters are so cute and so detailed, and of course, the last drop is great."

You must be at least 40 inches tall to ride.

HOT TIP!

If you sit in the front at Splash Mountain, you get really wet!

"The bears are great, and some of them are funny."

Brian L. (age 12)

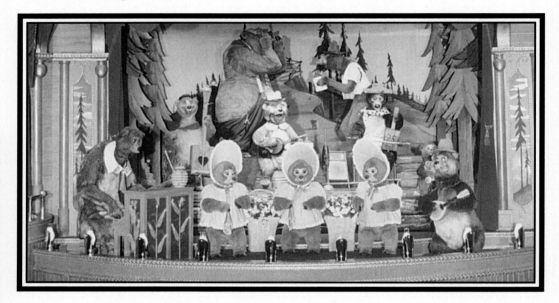

Country Bear Jamboree

You've never seen bears quite like these. They sing songs, play instruments, and tell jokes. This is a silly show, so be sure to go in with a silly attitude. Big Al is one of the most popular bears. He can't even carry a tune!

Everyone gets in on the act

Sometimes the audience sings and claps along with the performers. Even the furry heads on the wall get into the act. (Melvin the moose, Buff the buffalo, and Buck the deer like to *hang* around the theater.)

What do kids think of the bears?

The country music show gets mixed reviews from kids. Some love it. Others hate it. "It's strictly for little kids," says Lissy.

Karyn agrees, giving the show a rating of "two thumbs down and a couple of toes. But I think some kids would like to sing along with the characters," she adds.

Brian L. thinks "the bears are great, and some of them are funny. The one that can't sing is really funny. It's a very enjoyable show."

Tom Sawyer Island is quiet, but it's still rockin'—Teeter-Totter rock is a fun surprise to search for.

Tom Sawyer Island

There's only one way to get to Tom Sawyer Island—by raft. That's the way Tom himself used to travel. (He is a character created by the author Mark Twain.)

Don't expect to find any rides here. In fact, compared to the rest of the Magic Kingdom, it's pretty calm. But if you bring your imagination, you can have exciting adventures.

Bouncy bridges and secret exits

The island has a real windmill to wander through, hills to climb, and two neat bridges. One of them is an old barrel bridge. When one person bounces on it, everyone does.

Across one bridge is a wooden fort. It has air guns that you can shoot. And there's a secret exit that is really a path through a cave.

In all, there are three caves to explore. They are the best things on the island. Beware: The caves are very dark and a little scary.

Younger kids love it here

Tom Sawyer Island is popular with younger kids. Some older kids think it's dull. "The bridges and caves are fun, but the rest is boring," says Adam W., who is 14.

If you get hungry, stop by Aunt Polly's Dockside Inn for a snack. The pickles are delicious!

Who am I?

- I'm one of a kind
- I live in the Hundred Acre Wood
- I bounce!

Answer: Tigger

Big Thunder Mountain Railroad

Hang on, because this is one of the wildest rides in the wilderness. The speedy trains zip in, out, and over a huge mountain. They pass through scenes with real-looking chickens, goats, donkeys, and more.

The swoops and turns make this a thrilling roller coaster, but it's a lot tamer than Space Mountain. It's a ride you can go on again and again, and see new things each time. Look for funny sights in the town—like the poor guy floating around in a bathtub. Try to ride during the day and again at night.

Scream your head off

Kids have good things to say about this ride. "It's full of twists and turns," says Tate. Justin says, "It's not too scary, but I was screaming because it's so much fun."

More Frontierland Fun!

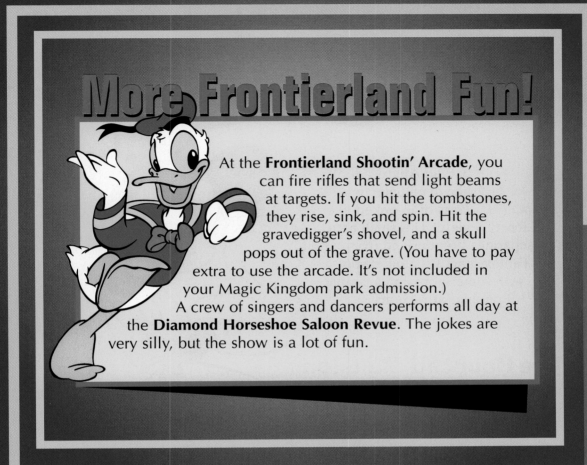

At the **Frontierland Shootin' Arcade**, you can fire rifles that send light beams at targets. If you hit the tombstones, they rise, sink, and spin. Hit the gravedigger's shovel, and a skull pops out of the grave. (You have to pay extra to use the arcade. It's not included in your Magic Kingdom park admission.) A crew of singers and dancers performs all day at the **Diamond Horseshoe Saloon Revue**. The jokes are very silly, but the show is a lot of fun.

A calmer coaster

Michael points out, "This ride is different than most roller coasters, so it's fun for me. The dips aren't that steep. And the speed is great!"

Szasha says, "Even if this is your first time, check out the scenery. There's a whole lot of things you might miss." Danielle T. agrees.

"There are all kinds of things to look at. I really liked the cave with all the bats," she says.

The kids like all the surprises on the ride. Dan says, "It's cool how it looks like you will hit something and then you go under it!"

You must be at least 40 inches tall to ride.

Liberty Square

What did America look like in colonial days? Parts of it looked like Liberty Square! This small area separates Frontierland from Fantasyland. It's a quiet spot with some shops and a couple of popular attractions.

The Haunted Mansion

This haunted house isn't too scary, but there are plenty of ghosts to keep you on your toes. Before you enter, read the funny tombstones outside. (We love the one that says: Here lies brother Fred. A great big rock fell on his head.)

Once inside, you'll be stranded in a room with no windows and no doors. For a while, it seems like there's no way out.

You are doomed

There's a moment before you board your "Doom Buggy" when the room is totally dark. It only lasts a few seconds, but for some, it's much too long.

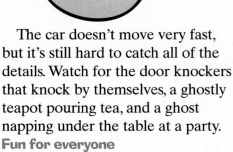

The car doesn't move very fast, but it's still hard to catch all of the details. Watch for the door knockers that knock by themselves, a ghostly teapot pouring tea, and a ghost napping under the table at a party.

Fun for everyone

This ride is popular with people of all ages. "It's awesome!" says Lissy. And, as Robbie says, "there's no real reason to be scared. The ride is more funny than scary."

The Hall of Presidents

The first part of this attraction is a film about our government. Then the screen rises and all of the American presidents are on the stage together. They are Audio-Animatronics, but they look real. Can you find President Bill Clinton in the photo above?

Abraham Lincoln and Bill Clinton actually speak. (Mr. Clinton recorded the voice himself. Abraham Lincoln's voice is performed by an actor.) If you watch closely, you'll notice the presidents move, whisper, and even doze off.

The kids were pleasantly surprised by this attraction. Danielle G. says, "I thought it would be boring, but it isn't." Lindsay agrees. "It's a fun way to learn," she says.

Liberty Belle Riverboat

The Liberty Belle Riverboat docks in Liberty Square. The big steamboat takes guests on slow, relaxing cruises. It can be a nice break on a hot day. The best seats are right up front or in the back, where you can see both sides of the river as you go along.

Mickey's Toontown Fair

Looking for that world-famous mouse? You're sure to find him at Mickey's Toontown Fair. He has a job here and, of course, he does it well.

This is the newest land in the Magic Kingdom. It must be a great place because Mickey, Minnie, and their friends all have country homes here. Everywhere you look, you see colorful tents. That's because the county fair is always in town. Guess who's the head judge. (Hint: Think of the Mouse who does a good job.)

To get here, follow the path from the Mad Tea Party or from Space Mountain. Or take a ride on the Walt Disney World Railroad. It's a short trip and, if you ask Michael, it's worth it. "I think all kids will like it here," he says.

The Barnstormer

The only ride in Toontown Fair is the roller coaster at Goofy's Wiseacre Farm. The ride may look small, but it packs plenty of thrills. "I like the part where you go sideways really fast," Szasha says.

If you climb into a "plane," you'll zip through the farm. But watch out! You're about to crash into Goofy's barn. The hole in the wall tells you that someone has been there before you. Yes, it's clumsy old Goofy.

Before you ride, explore Goofy's farm. Some of his vegetables are pretty wacky, just like him. Keep your eye out for the "bell" peppers and the "pop" corn. Then look up. Only Goofy would park his airplane in a water tower!

Toon Park

In the center of Toontown Fair is a playground. Parents can rest while young kids check out the animals. They're made of foam and great for climbing. They oink (and moo or neigh) when you poke them.

HOT

Mickey's Toontown Fair is a great place to meet the characters.

TIP

Donald's Boat

A popular stop in Toontown is Donald's Boat. It's called the *SS Miss Daisy* and it's full of leaks. When you pull the whistle, water shoots out the top. To get to the boat, cross the "duck pond"—another great spot to get wet.

Mickey's Country House

The door is open, so come on in! Mickey's house tells you a lot about him. His game room is full of sports stuff. But the kitchen is a mess. That's what happens when you let Donald and Goofy decorate!

Where's Mickey? He's hard at work in the Judge's Tent. Walk out the back door of the house and follow the path. You can't miss it! On your way, check out Mickey's garden. Even the vegetables have mouse ears.

Judge's Tent

You found him! Mickey is here all day long, ready to have his picture taken with you. There's always a wait, but the line is shorter late in the day.

Minnie's Country House

Go ahead, climb on the furniture—Minnie won't mind. There's lots to see and touch in this house. Press the button on Minnie's answering machine and listen to her messages. Open the refrigerator, and feel the cold air. And get set for a trick when you try to take a chocolate chip cookie off her table.

Danielle T. loves Minnie's house "because it's so interactive. There are all sorts of things to do in the kitchen. It's not roped off like Mickey's," she says.

Once you've explored inside, head for Minnie's backyard. She hangs out there sometimes. On your way there, look at the funny flowers in the sun room. The palm tree has hands, the tiger lilies have tiger faces, and the tulips all have two lips!

Toontown Hall of Fame

This tent is filled with winning entries from the fair. But the best reason to come here is to meet the characters. In one room, shake hands with old favorites, including Goofy, Pluto, Chip, and Dale. Pooh and his pals are in another room. Newer Disney stars like Belle, Hercules, and Mulan appear here, too.

Disney Discoveries

It's easy to find fun things to see and do in Walt Disney World. It's a little harder to find them in this puzzle. They're hidden. The words are written forward, backward, across, up, down, and diagonally. Draw a circle around each word as you discover it.

Animals
Boats
Castle
Chip
Dinosaurs
Dragon
Fireworks
Ghost
Mickey
Monorail
Movies
Parade
Parks
Pirates
Teacup

```
S E T A R I P S O F
K M S C A S T L E I
R O O T E A C U P R
A V H N O C A S T E
P I G B O P I H C W
R E O P A R A D E O
E S A N I M A L S R
T N O G A R D I H K
A M I C K E Y P L S
W S R U A S O N I D
```

Fantasyland

Fantasyland is home to a lot of magical rides that younger kids just love. Older kids and even grown-ups enjoy them, too. These attractions are very popular, but the lines are usually shorter while people are watching the afternoon parade. So it's a good idea to skip the parade one day and visit Fantasyland. Plan to catch the parade on another day.

Kids who remember the 20,000 Leagues Under the Sea attraction should know that it's closed. A new ride may open at that spot in the future.

Ariel's Grotto

There is a mysterious blue cave tucked behind Dumbo the Flying Elephant. Inside, there is a special surprise—and her name is Ariel. The star of *The Little Mermaid* is waiting to meet you in her grotto (grotto is another word for cave). Don't forget to bring a camera and an autograph book.

Out front, there are some fountains to play in, so it's a great place to get wet.

Szasha says, "If you really like Ariel, you should definitely go." She also likes the "funny rocks that squirt water." Danielle T. has this advice: "Try to go when it's not so crowded, or you may have to wait a long time."

"You can never grow too old for a carousel."

Lissy (age 11)

Cinderella's Golden Carrousel

Just about all of the attractions at Walt Disney World were dreamed up by Disney Imagineers. But not the carousel. It was discovered in New Jersey, where it was once part of another amusement park. It was built around 1917.

When you climb on a horse for your ride on the carousel, be sure to notice that each one is different. And remember to look up at the ceiling and its hand-painted scenes from *Cinderella*. While you ride, enjoy famous Disney tunes, including "Zip-A-Dee-Doo-Dah," "When You Wish Upon a Star," and "Be Our Guest."

"You can never grow too old for a carousel," says Lissy. "The horses are beautiful and the music makes it great." Robert agrees. "I love the carousel and I love the music. I think people of any age would like it."

"You can go as fast or as slow as you want."

Brian L. (age 12)

Mad Tea Party

The idea for the giant teacups that spin through this ride came from a scene in *Alice in Wonderland*. In the movie, the Mad Hatter throws himself a tea party to celebrate his un-birthday. That's any day that *isn't* his birthday!

You control the spin

On the Mad Tea Party ride, you control how fast your cup spins by turning the big wheel in the center. The more you turn, the more you spin. Or you can just sit back and let the cup spin on its own. It may be hard while you're whirling, but try to take a peek at the little mouse who keeps popping out of the big teapot in the center.

"It's a very good ride and it really makes you dizzy," says Nita. Brian L. agrees. "I wish it would go even faster, but it's good that you can go as fast or as slow as you want," he says.

It takes teamwork

For the best ride, David suggests that everyone in the cup try to work together. "You have to coordinate," he says. "Sometimes you can go faster if fewer people work at spinning the wheel."

Most kids agree that the ride is too short (it lasts about two minutes). Lissy doesn't mind, though. "Your arms get tired after a while," says Lissy, "but the teacups are always fun."

Dumbo the Flying Elephant

Just like the star of the movie *Dumbo*, these elephants know how to fly. They'd love to take you for a short ride (about two minutes) above Fantasyland. A button lets you control the up and down movement of the elephant.

Take your kid brother

Many of the kids agree that this ride is more fun for younger kids from ages 3 to 8. But they all find something to like, and think it would be fun to go on with a younger brother or sister.

Brian L. also suggests it for younger kids. "It's not a bad ride, and I think little kids would love it," he says. Robert likes "to go up really high. I think some kids might be scared of the height, though."

Beware of long lines

Even though Disney added more Dumbos a few years ago, lines for this attraction tend to be long. Anna thinks the ride is "way too short. But if you don't wait in line too long, it's fun to go on."

Danielle G. loves it. "It has the appearance of a child's ride, but it's fun for everyone," she says. Tate agrees. "Most people think it's just for little kids, but it's fun."

"I never get tired of this ride."

David (age 13)

Peter Pan's Flight

Swoop and soar through scenes that tell the story of how Wendy, Michael, and John get sprinkled with pixie dust and fly off to Never Land with Peter Pan and Tinker Bell. Along the way you meet up with Princess Tiger Lily, the evil Captain Hook, and his sidekick Mr. Smee.

Near the beginning of the trip, there's a beautiful scene of London at night. Notice that the cars on the streets really move. Later, watch out for the crocodile who wants to eat Captain Hook.

When you first board your pirate ship, it seems like you're riding on a track on the ground. Once you get going the track is actually above you, so it feels like the ship is really flying.

"I love this ride and how it makes you feel like you can fly," says Robert. "I especially like the part at the end with the crocodile."

Ashley P. thinks "the city scene is neat with all the cars going up and down. I also like how it's so dark."

David points out that Peter Pan's Flight is different from all the other Fantasyland rides because "you're hooked from the top instead of being on a track below you." He adds, "I never get tired of this ride."

It's a Small World

People have a lot in common, no matter where they live. That's the point of this attraction. In it, you take a slow boat ride through several large rooms where beautiful dolls represent different parts of the world. There are Greek dancers, Japanese kite flyers, Scottish bagpipers, and many more. There's also a jungle scene with hippos, giraffes, and monkeys.

All this colorful scenery is set to the song "It's a Small World." Pay attention to the costumes on the dolls, and try to guess which country they're from. Nita says, "The costumes are adorable, and I like the faces on the dolls. But the ride is too slow. If it had a few dips, it would be better."

Lissy agrees that the ride is a little slow, but "it's really pretty and there are so many neat things to look at that it doesn't matter."

Ashley P. thinks the song gets a little tiring. "I really like the costumes and cultures, but the song just keeps playing over and over."

As for David, "I don't hate it, but I do think it's better for younger kids," he says.

Mr. Toad's Wild Ride

Mr. Toad is not a very good driver. So when you hop into one of his cars heading to "Nowhere in Particular," you're in for a wild trip. The cars go zigging and zagging around sharp turns. You crash through a fireplace, just miss being hit by a falling suit of armor, go through haystacks, and then ride down a railroad track. Watch out for the speeding train!

Most of the kids agree that Mr. Toad's Wild Ride is for younger kids, although there are a few scary moments that might frighten them.

"It's good for young kids," says Karyn. "It's pretty boring for someone my age." David agrees that it's a kiddie ride. "Some of the characters are funny, but it's really for younger kids," he says. "I don't like that many of the characters are made out of cardboard."

But Lissy thinks the scenery is "neat and I like how they have everything moving. When I saw the train coming, it was a little scary," she says. Robert agrees. "It sort of scared me little bit," he says.

"The witch hops out so close to you."

Ashley P. (age 11)

Snow White's Adventures

This attraction takes you through scenes from the movie *Snow White and the Seven Dwarfs*. Some scenes are sweet, while others are scary. If you like Snow White, you're in luck. She is in a lot of scenes (but so is the nasty old witch). Don't expect to see much of the dwarfs—they don't show up a lot.

There are lots of turns, and the witch seems to be around each one of them. It's very dark during most of the ride, so it can get pretty creepy—especially for younger kids.

The kids aren't sure who this ride is meant for. It's too scary for many small children and a little boring for older kids.

Karyn says, "There should be more happy parts in it." Ashley P. doesn't mind the scary parts as much. "The witch hops out so close to you," she says. Brian L. likes that some scenes are like the movie, but he agrees that "little kids would be terrified seeing the wicked witch." What do *you* think?

45

"I was mesmerized the whole time."

Dawna (age 11)

Legend of the Lion King

Disney's hit movie comes to life in Legend of the Lion King. This show uses animation, life-size puppets, special effects, and music to tell the story of Simba and his friends from the movie.

When the sun rises over Pride Rock, Mufasa and Simba make their big entrance. The characters may look life-like, but they are really large puppets.

Sing "Hakuna Matata"

As the story continues, other characters act out parts of the movie. Special effects, like water mists and wind, make the theater seem like a jungle. During the stampede scene, the room rumbles. Of course, no Lion King show would be complete without a visit from Timon and Pumbaa. When they sing "Hakuna Matata," feel free to sing along!

Kids agree

All the kids agree that this is a great show. Dan says he loves all the special effects, "like the steam shooting up on the stage and the light rain."

"It's the best play I've ever seen," says Michael. Dawna agrees. "This has to be the best show anywhere. I was mesmerized the whole time."

Skyway to Tomorrowland

Drifting along in a Skyway car is the next best thing to flying. The ride lifts guests high in the air above the Magic Kingdom. It runs between Fantasyland and Tomorrowland. All trips are one-way.

"It's fun," says Lindsay. "You get a really good view of the park and you can take pictures."

Dawna and Danielle G. both think the ride feels like a ski lift. Dawna offers this tip: "It's not a good ride if you're afraid of heights."

The Skyway is a popular ride with a slow-moving line. If you're in a rush, there's a much faster way to get places—your feet!

Tomorrowland

Tomorrowland began as a peek at the future. But as the real world changed, so did this land. Now, it's like a city from a science fiction story. The rides here let you rocket through space or travel through time. The palm trees are made of metal. And a scary alien even beams down for a visit! A good way to see this land is to ride on the Tomorrowland Transit Authority—it's cool and breezy and it never has a line.

Space Mountain

Roller coaster fans like to head straight for this rocket ride through outer space. It has twists, turns, and steep dips. And it all takes place in the dark! It's one of the most popular rides in the park.

Older kids love it

Danielle T. says, "I really felt like I was in a rocket going to space. This is one of the best rides." Dan agrees. "I like how they put you in the dark with all the planets," he says.

Nita has a warning: "It goes too fast. I'm not a roller coaster person, and I felt like I was about to fall out."

Is it too scary?

Everyone agrees: Space Mountain is scary! But some kids say it's a "good scary." Anything that was "bad scary" happened only in their imaginations.

Anna says, "The ride rattles a lot. I wish that there were sides to the cars." But don't worry: The coaster is perfectly safe. And, as Amy says, "It just wouldn't be a trip to Disney World without riding it!"

You must be 44 inches tall to ride.

HOT
Never eat right before going on Space Mountain.
TIP

"You'll scream until you can scream no more!"

Ashley J. (age 12)

The ExtraTERRORestrial Alien Encounter

People from another planet want to show off their new machine. They say it can beam people through space. But that's not what happens. Instead, an alien arrives and escapes into the audience. It's ugly and it's hungry. And it just might eat *you*!

It's not for everyone

That's the story of Alien Encounter, the Magic Kingdom's scariest attraction. Kids like this show a lot but say that it's not for everyone—especially younger kids. "The first time I went on it I was 10 and I cried," says Amy. "But I've always been a scaredy cat."

Brian F. says, "I did not go on it, because I don't like aliens. I went to the arcade instead." Lindsay feels just the opposite. She likes scary things and loves this attraction.

The alien licks your head

Adam F. likes the effects. "They show the alien in front of you. Then the lights go off and it feels like it's breathing and slobbering on you."

Ashley J. says, "When the alien gets out, you'll scream until you can scream no more!"

You must be at least 44 inches tall to enter Alien Encounter.

The Timekeeper

Travel through time with Timekeeper, one of the world's wackiest robots. In this attraction, he takes you on a tour of the past and the future.

Okay, you don't *really* time travel in this attraction—but it feels like you do. A robot named 9-Eye is the real time traveler. She takes pictures that fill the nine screens in the theater. A movie completely surrounds the audience.

It will make your head spin

When you watch the screens, it feels like you're moving. (There are no seats in the theater.)

"This made me dizzy," says Lindsay. "But it still is sort of neat." Dawna agrees. "This is a very funny show. If there's a line, it would be worth the wait."

Don't miss it

Seth says he enjoyed taking a "ride in a time machine with a crazed robot." He has a tip: "Don't forget to look behind you." Otherwise you might miss something.

Arcade Alert!

The **Tomorrowland Light & Power Co.** is a high-tech video arcade. It's right next to Space Mountain.

It's a good place to wait if you don't want to ride Space Mountain or go to Alien Encounter. Just like other arcades, you have to pay to play here.

Walt Disney's Carousel of Progress

A lot has changed since 1900. There was no electricity, water came from a well, and nobody had a TV. Life was rough! This attraction shows you how life has changed since then.

A look at American families

The show is called Carousel of Progress because you move in a circle, just like on a carousel. You pass different scenes along the way. Each one teaches a little history.

"I really appreciate the story," says Tate. "It's a down-to-earth look at how the American family has progressed over the years."

Learning can be fun

Anna finds it "a good way to learn. I think it's cool when they say, in the early scenes, how 'that will never happen,' and we know that it already has."

Adam W. likes "how we learn about all the inventions that were created in the years past."

Brad's favorite is "the part at the end when the granny is playing the virtual reality game. The last scene is the best."

Have you ever been to the Carousel of Progress? Do you have a favorite scene?

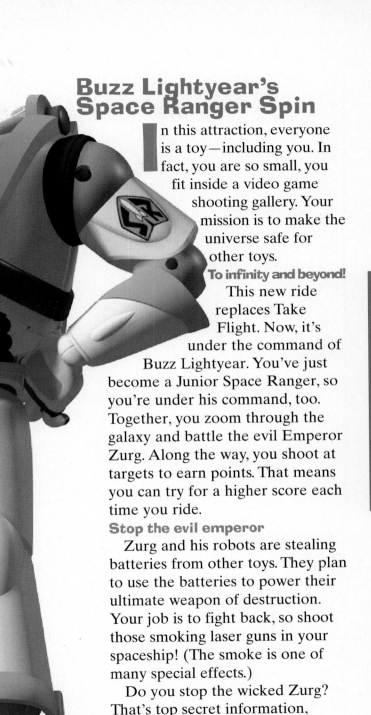

Buzz Lightyear's Space Ranger Spin

In this attraction, everyone is a toy—including you. In fact, you are so small, you fit inside a video game shooting gallery. Your mission is to make the universe safe for other toys.

To infinity and beyond!

This new ride replaces Take Flight. Now, it's under the command of Buzz Lightyear. You've just become a Junior Space Ranger, so you're under his command, too. Together, you zoom through the galaxy and battle the evil Emperor Zurg. Along the way, you shoot at targets to earn points. That means you can try for a higher score each time you ride.

Stop the evil emperor

Zurg and his robots are stealing batteries from other toys. They plan to use the batteries to power their ultimate weapon of destruction. Your job is to fight back, so shoot those smoking laser guns in your spaceship! (The smoke is one of many special effects.)

Do you stop the wicked Zurg? That's top secret information, unless you're a Space Ranger.

Magic Kingdom

Tomorrowland Speedway

You don't need a license to drive your own car around this racetrack (as long as you're 52 inches tall). Cars travel along a track, but it's not as easy to drive as it looks. Even experts bounce around a lot. The cars are real and are powered by gasoline.

Some of the kids really enjoy driving their own cars. "The race cars are fun because you get to steer them yourself," says Szasha. "I like the curves." Robert says, "I love it. I think it goes pretty fast and I like having my own car."

Karyn think the race cars could be a little more exciting. David agrees. "I like the ride," he says. "But I wish they didn't have the track in the middle."

Astro Orbiter

In the middle of Tomorrowland, there is a giant, glowing tower. It is called Rockettower. The Astro Orbiter ride is all the way at the top. In it, you soar past colorful planets high above Tomorrowland.

You can take the ride by yourself or with a friend. (Each rocket fits two people.) "This is a ride that everyone will enjoy," says Tate. "It's fast, but not too scary." Dawna says, "People who don't have the stomach for Space Mountain can go. It still has the space theme."

Kirsti has a tip: "Sit in the front so you can control how high up you go."

Take a Tour of Tomorrowland!

The **Tomorrowland Transit Authority** travels by or through most of the land's attractions. If you're not sure about going on Space Mountain, the view from here can help you decide. It's also interesting that the ride doesn't give off any pollution. Szasha says, "It takes you past the different rides so you can see what they are like before riding them." Dawna says, "You can see a lot of Tomorrowland in a very short time." Michael adds, "The announcer tells you about each ride. And it's a good place to rest."

If you would like to ride the **Skyway** cable cars that travel between Tomorrowland and Fantasyland, this is the best place to board. The lines at the Tomorrowland station are much shorter, so get on here.

Entertainment

The Magic Kingdom is a very entertaining place. It seems like there is always a show starting or a parade going by. Read on to learn about some of the special events that take place in the park. For more information, check a park guidemap. You can get one in any Disney resort, at the entrance to the park, or in the shops and restaurants.

SPECTROMAGIC

This parade makes its way down Main Street twice each night during busy seasons. Special lighting effects and lots of characters make for a show that, as Dawna says, "no one should miss. It's a perfect way to end an evening or a trip."

DISNEY'S MAGICAL MOMENTS PARADE

Your favorite Disney characters are on the march in this parade. Mickey and his pals want everyone to join in the fun. Danielle T. says, "I danced in the Cinderella scene. It was an experience I'll never forget!"

Each parade float has a surprise, like confetti or fireworks. Szasha has a tip: "Get a spot on the curb early. They may ask you to be in the parade."

FANTASY IN THE SKY FIREWORKS

Look—up in the sky! It's not a bird or a plane . . . it's the most amazing fireworks show you've ever seen! Hundreds of colorful bursts explode within seven minutes. For the best view of the show, stand right in the middle of Main Street, facing the castle.

Where to Find Characters at the Magic Kingdom

Disney characters greet guests all over the Magic Kingdom. The best place to find them is **Mickey's Toontown Fair**. You can meet Mickey in the **Judge's Tent**, and the rest of the gang in the **Toontown Hall of Fame**.

Rafiki and Timon like to hang out at the entrance to **Adventureland**. Alice and her friends prefer **Fantasyland**, while Brer Fox and Brer Bear enjoy spending time at **Splash Mountain**.

If you want to meet The Little Mermaid, go to **Ariel's Grotto** in Fantasyland. There are lots of fountains you can play in, too.

To find out exactly where and when to meet your favorite characters, pick up a free park guidemap or ask a cast member.

MAGIC KINGDOM TIPS

If the park is open late, it's fun to go on your favorite attractions again after dark.

Head to this park first, since it has the most rides for kids.

Arrive a half hour before the opening time. Walk down Main Street to get a head start for when the rest of the park opens.

Check the Tip Boards on Main Street, in Frontierland, and in Tomorrowland. They list the wait times for popular attractions.

Thrill rides like Space Mountain and Splash Mountain and all of the Fantasyland rides are usually very crowded. Lines are shorter in the early morning, late in the evening, and during parades.

Need to cool off on a hot day? Stop by Ariel's Grotto in Fantasyland, Donald's Boat in Mickey's Toontown Fair, or Cool Ship in Tomorrowland. You can get soaked with water at all of these places.

There are "chicken exits" in the line for Space Mountain, just in case you change your mind about riding at the last minute.

Never eat just before riding The Barnstormer, Astro Orbiter, Space Mountain, Big Thunder Mountain Railroad, or the Mad Tea Party.

If you've never been on a roller coaster, ride The Barnstormer first. If you like it, try Big Thunder Mountain Railroad next. Save Space Mountain for last—it's the scariest.

If there are two lines at an attraction, the one on the left is usually shorter.

Attraction Ratings

COOL
(Check It Out)

- Dumbo the Flying Elephant
- Cinderella's Golden Carrousel
- Skyway
- Snow White's Adventures
- The Hall of Presidents
- The Timekeeper
- Tomorrowland Transit Authority
- Walt Disney World Railroad
- Liberty Belle Riverboat
- Swiss Family Treehouse

REALLY COOL
(Don't Miss)

- The Barnstormer
- Astro Orbiter
- Tomorrowland Speedway
- The Enchanted Tiki Room—Under New Management
- Mad Tea Party
- Country Bear Jamboree
- Jungle Cruise
- It's a Small World
- Carousel of Progress
- Tom Sawyer Island
- Mr. Toad's Wild Ride

THE COOLEST
(See at Least Twice)

- Space Mountain
- Splash Mountain
- Big Thunder Mountain Railroad
- The Haunted Mansion
- Peter Pan's Flight
- Alien Encounter
- Buzz Lightyear's Space Ranger Spin
- Pirates of the Caribbean
- Legend of the Lion King

Magic Kingdom

What do YOU think?

The kids who worked on this book rated all the attractions at Walt Disney World. But your opinion counts, too! Make your own "Attraction Ratings" list for each park and send it to us. We'll use it when we create next year's book. (Our address is on page 6.)

Epcot

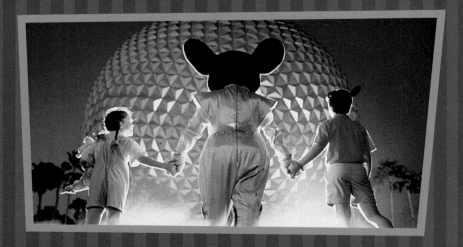

Epcot is a great place to make discoveries about the world. At this theme park, things that used to seem ordinary suddenly become fun. All of the attractions at Epcot are in buildings called pavilions. The pavilions are in two sections of the park. One section is **Future World**, and the other is **World Showcase**. Future World celebrates cool inventions and ideas. It shows how they affect everything, from the land and sea to your mind and body.

World Showcase lets you travel around the world without leaving the park! There are 11 different countries to visit here. Each country has copies of its famous buildings, restaurants, and other landmarks. Together, they make you feel as if you're visiting the real place.

FRANCE
MOROCCO
JAPAN
THE AMERICAN ADVENTURE
ITALY
GERMANY
CHINA
NORWAY
MEXICO

INTERNATIONAL GATEWAY
UNITED KINGDOM
AMERICA GARDENS THEATRE
WORLD SHOWCASE LAGOON

CANADA
JOURNEY INTO IMAGINATION
THE LAND
SHOWCASE PLAZA
INNOVENTIONS WEST
THE LIVING SEAS
INNOVENTIONS EAST
TEST TRACK
HORIZONS
SPACESHIP EARTH
WONDERS OF LIFE
UNIVERSE OF ENERGY
Entrance Plaza
To Buses

N

Epcot is a big place. Use this map to help plan your trip through the park.

Future World

When you enter Epcot by monorail, you are in the area called Future World. Many of the attractions here are educational—but that doesn't mean you won't have fun. Take it from the kids: There's a lot to explore.

SPACESHIP EARTH

You can't miss the silver ball that is the symbol of Epcot. It's gigantic. The Spaceship Earth ride is inside this big, round building. The ride shows you the different ways people have communicated over the years.

A highlight of the trip is when your time machine vehicle reaches the top of the building. Look up and you'll think you are staring into a night sky. The stars are beautiful.

Older kids enjoy this attraction more than younger ones do. Ashley P. didn't like the ride when she was younger, but "now it's much more interesting to me," she says.

Nita says, "The details are great, like the monk who is snoring."

After the ride, check out the AT&T Global Neighborhood. There are games and other fun activities. Don't miss the TV that listens to you when you speak.

INNOVENTIONS

Here's your chance to test some exciting new inventions. You may also surf the Internet, try out some brand-new video games, or see (and smell) cookies baked in a high-tech way.

Innoventions fills two buildings in Future Word. New inventions are brought in every three months or so. As Ashley J. says, "The place changes all the time, so you can come again and again." But no matter when you come, you'll get a taste of the future.

Adam F. says, "I wanted to try virtual reality, but the exhibits were too crowded." Instead, he tested some computers. One of them even understood him when he talked to it!

Dan was more interested in an exhibit about flying. "I like how you can see the inside of an airplane engine," he says. "I always wondered how they worked."

Danielle T. would "plan on spending several hours here." So would Seth. "You can never get bored here," he says.

"It feels like you're going way down to the bottom of the sea."

Robert (age 8)

THE LIVING SEAS

There's something fishy about the animals at The Living Seas. They aren't like any of the other animals in Future World. These critters are all real!

There are more than 8,000 sea creatures living here. It's the world's largest aquarium. There are turtles, dolphins, manatees, and even sharks.

Under the sea

Your sea exploration begins with a short movie. It explains how the earth's oceans were formed. Next, you get in a "hydrolator" (an elevator that goes in water) to go down to see the aquarium. As you get out, ask your parents how deep they think the hydrolator went. Then tell them it moved less than one inch!

Hands-on fun

After a quick ride through the aquarium, you enter an area called Sea Base Alpha. This is your chance to take a closer look at the creatures and to try out the hands-on exhibits.

"The Living Seas is really cool," says Robert. "I thought my ears popped in the hydrolator. It feels like you're going way down to the bottom of the sea."

Brian L. likes the interactive exhibits. "You can put your arms in a diving suit and try to move like you're in the ocean," he says.

Karyn just loves the manatees. "The rest of the exhibits are okay," she says, "but I like to see animals."

"The greenhouses are amazing."

Lindsay (age 9)

THE LAND

The building called The Land looks like a big greenhouse. The attractions inside focus on food and where it comes from. There's a boat ride, a funny show about food, and special guided tours. There's also a movie about the environment. It stars Simba, Timon, and Pumbaa from *The Lion King*.

Living with the Land

What's the most popular fruit on our planet? The banana! People eat more bananas than any other fruity snack. You'll learn lots more food facts on this boat trip. The boat travels through rooms that look like a rain forest, desert, and prairie. Then it heads to a greenhouse area.

A tour guide explains everything your boat floats past. If you're lucky, you'll see some giant vegetables growing here. The greenhouse has produced some of the biggest lemons and eggplants in the world!

In all, The Land grows more than 30 tons of fruit and veggies each year. A lot of it is served to guests in Epcot restaurants.

This boat ride scores high marks with kids. Lindsay says, "The greenhouses are amazing." Anna likes that "it shows us new ways to make the best of our earth."

Behind the Seeds Tour

Kids (and parents) who are interested in the environment can sign up for this one-hour guided tour of the growing areas at The Land. It costs $6 for adults and $4 for kids ages 3 through 9. You'll need reservations. Make them at the front of the Green Thumb Emporium shop.

Food Rocks

Here's a different kind of rock concert with a lesson about good nutrition. These are performers you won't see on any other stage. They are popular musicians who have been turned into foods. They perform old songs with funny new words.

Follow your nose

In the pre-show area, look at the fun food facts painted on the walls. Open one of the "smell boxes" and get a strong whiff of chocolate, garlic, coffee, bacon, orange, or seafood. Dawna points out the carpeting, with its pattern of forks, knives, and spoons.

Eat right—or else!

Kids enjoy this show, but it's best for a younger audience. "This is a good way to teach kids about the right foods to eat," says Lindsay. Tate thinks Food Rocks is "a cute show for young kids." Dawna thinks the show "makes you feel guilty for eating food that's not good for you."

Most of the kids like the names of the performers and the songs they sing. But sometimes it's hard to make out the lyrics. "I can't understand all the words of the songs," Lindsay says. "I do think their names are clever, though."

The Circle of Life

Simba, Timon, and Pumbaa are together again. This time they're in a movie about protecting the earth's environment. The film is a mix of animation and live action. It shows some of the problems we face — and how we can fix them.

Timber!

The movie's opening scene shows animals just like those in *The Lion King* (but these animals are real). Next you see Simba near a watering hole. All of a sudden he hears "Timber!" and is drenched by the splash of a tree falling into water. Timon and Pumbaa are clearing the grassland to build a resort (The Hakuna Matata Lakeside Village).

Simba tells a story

Simba remembers what his father taught him about caring for the land. He tells his friends a story about how humans sometimes forget that everything is connected in the great Circle of Life.

Brian F. gets the message of this film. "It means to recycle, don't pollute, and don't litter," he explains. "I like the pictures they took of the fish, birds, alligators, penguins, and bears. And the cartoons are funny."

For Emma, "this movie is a nice reminder about what happens when we forget about the Circle of Life." Ashley J. says, "It really makes you want to change everything. I'm going to recycle more!"

JOURNEY INTO IMAGINATION

Your host at this pavilion is Figment—a magical creature who looks like a little purple dragon. There are many things to do inside this building. There is a ride through the wonders of the imagination, a hands-on activity center called Image Works, and a wacky 3-D movie called Honey, I Shrunk the Audience.

Don't miss the special surprises *outside* the building. They're called Leap Frog Fountains. Everyone is amazed by the streams of water that leap from one garden to another. There are a lot of other ways to have fun here, too. Just use your imagination!

Journey into Imagination Ride

This attraction is a tour of the imagination. The ride shows you how powerful your imagination really is. Figment and his friend Dreamfinder are the guides for the trip. They explain how the five senses (sight, smell, sound, touch, and taste) send messages to the brain. Those messages help you create dreams and ideas.

It's all in your head

Many kids enjoy the imagination ride, but it isn't one of their favorites. Lindsay thinks the scenery is "very creative. You keep seeing the dragon and what he's imagining." Anna's favorite part is that "they show you all the cool things you can do with art, like the sparkles, holograms, paints, and lights."

But Adam W. thinks the ride is too long. "It's a little boring," he says. Tate agrees. "Although it does have a lot of neat stuff to look at," he adds.

"If you stand in the right place (near the fountains), you can get totally wet."

Taran (age 9)

Leap Frog Fountains

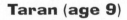t's easy to guess where these fountains get their name. Streams of water leap from one garden spot to the next with no clear pattern. Catch them if you can!

This area is a hit with kids of all ages. "If you stand in the right place, you can get totally wet," says Taran. "It's one of my favorite things."

Nita thinks it's neat "how the water jumps right over your head." Brian F. has "never seen fountains do that before. They really do look like they're leaping over each other."

"Image Works has everything a kid could need to occupy herself."

Lissy (age 11)

Image Works

Once you get inside Image Works, it may be hard to leave. Kids love it because it's full of hands-on (and feet-on) activities. The Rainbow Corridor is a tunnel with neon tubes in all the colors of the rainbow. Walk through it and you'll reach Stepping Tones, where you step on colored lights to trigger different sounds.

The Magic Palette has a special pen and screen to create images. At the Electronic Philharmonic you can conduct an orchestra by raising and lowering your hands. And there's more!

"This place is awesome," says Lissy. "Image Works has everything a kid could need to occupy herself."

Nita agrees. "There's so much to do. My favorite is directing the band." Danielle T. likes the Making Faces computer. "You can make yourself look really crazy!" she says.

Honey, I Shrunk the Audience

Remember the kids from *Honey, I Shrunk the Kids*? This 3-D movie gives you an idea of how they felt. That's because this time, you're the one who gets shrunk, along with the rest of the audience. Even the theater seems to shrink.

You get spooked by 3-D mice, a lion, and a scary snake. Then one of the kids from the movie picks up the theater and carries it around. Somehow you're brought back to real size, but only after some unusual adventures.

Very special effects

As Brian F. tells it, "First the professor shrinks himself. Then he accidentally hits the laser and shrinks us! The people on the screen are really big." Emma adds, "It makes you feel really small."

Brian F. says, "When the 3-D mice come out, it seems like they are really there. It's cool." Ashley J. also finds the effects believable. "I even put my feet up!" she says.

Some scary moments

"This is a very neat experience," says Lindsay. "But some parts might be scary for little kids."

Tate says, "This attraction really gives you the feeling that you're shrinking. There's a neat twist at the end." But we won't tell you what it is. As Emma puts it, "I don't want to give any more away. It's nice having a surprise."

TEST TRACK

What is it like to be a crash test dummy? Find out in this thrilling ride—and learn what new cars go through to be safe for riders.

Test Track is Epcot's fastest ride. It was not open when we visited, but we took kids on a special behind-the-scenes tour. (It was scheduled to open by early 1999.)

Where are the brakes?

The sporty test cars travel on a track that's almost a mile long. Your car has no steering wheel or brake pedals, but its sound and video equipment lets you know what's being tested. You zip around curves, zoom down a street, and bounce on bumpy roads. At one point, you nearly crash into a truck!

A crash course in car safety

Kids think this ride is a fun way to learn more about cars.

Dan says, "These cool test cars take you on a fast ride with sharp turns and sudden stops. The turns are great. I like going sideways."

Danielle T. says, "The banks on the curves are incredible. They look really steep. Only ride if you can handle it." Szasha agrees. "People with motion sickness should not ride," she says.

Michael says, "It's a fun, speedy, and scary ride. Lots of kids will like it because they like going fast."

Don't worry—it's safer than it looks. Disney workers tested all the cars first. After all, that's what test driving is all about. You must be at least 40 inches tall to try it.

HORIZONS

What do you predict for the future? Getting to school in a flying bus? Dancing on the ceiling of your bedroom? Or maybe, going to college on another planet? Anything is possible in the future! That is what this attraction is all about.

A look at the future

The ride takes place in a special car that travels sideways. It lets you get a good look at all the scenes as you pass them. The first area shows how people might communicate with each other in the future—by using high-tech telephones. Not only can you hear who's calling, but you see a holographic image of the person right in front of you.

Another scene shows how crops may someday grow in the dry, sandy desert. (This area smells like oranges!) There is also a part that shows what an underwater city might look like.

It's hard to predict the future, but one thing's for sure—there will always be new challenges and new problems to solve. (Including teaching robots to wash the dishes and getting dogs to walk themselves.)

Your vote counts

This attraction teaches us that people can work together to solve a lot of problems. For example, you will have to work with the people in your ride vehicle to make a big decision. Do you want to end your trip to the future by having an adventure on the land, in the sea, or in outer space? Everybody gets to vote—and majority rules.

What do kids think of this trip to the future and back?

"I like the part where you choose where you want to go," says Nita. "It should be longer, though, because it's very interesting."

David thinks there's a lot to see along the way. And he likes "learning about everyone's hopes for the future."

WONDERS OF LIFE

You know what you look like on the outside. Now find out what you look like on the inside. This pavilion is all about the human body. It's easy to spend a couple of hours here, so come early to beat the crowds.

Body Wars

Every time you get a cut, it's white blood cells to the rescue. They destroy infections and help you heal. In this attraction, white blood cells mistake a scientist for an infection. She was shrunk for a special mission inside a body—to remove a nasty splinter. Now the white blood cells are after her! Your mission is to rescue her before it's too late.

Go inside a body

This ride through the human body takes place in a room called a simulator. (It's like Star Tours at the Disney-MGM Studios.) Together, the simulator and a movie make you feel like you're inside another person.

A bumpy ride

Karyn says, "I like all the special effects, but it's too bumpy." Brian L. feels the same way. "You really get jerked around too much," he says.

The ride is still a favorite for most of the kids. "I love it," says Robert. "It's fun the way you go through the body." Ashley P. agrees. "I really like bumpy rides, so I like this one a lot."

 If the sight of blood makes you woozy, don't ride Body Wars.

Cranium Command

Imagine that you're a pilot. But instead of flying an airplane, you pilot the brain of a 12-year-old boy. That's what happens to Buzzy during this attraction, and you get to go along for the ride.

Buzzy and the brain

The pre-show is a funny cartoon that explains how Buzzy gets his job. Then you go into a theater—and inside the brain with Buzzy. You watch as he tries to get the parts of the brain to work together.

Kids identify with Bobby

The brain in Cranium Command belongs to a boy named Bobby. (The cranium is the part of your skull where your brain is.) It's Buzzy's job to pilot Bobby through a day at school. "I can relate to the things that happen to the boy in the story," says Tate. Can you?

Fitness Fairgrounds

The lobby of the pavilion has so many hands-on activities, the kids think you can spend at least an hour here.

Wonder Cycles are bikes that let you watch a film while riding. The faster you pedal, the faster the action in the film goes!

In the Coach's Corner, a computer checks your tennis, baseball, and golf swings and gives you tips for a better game. In the Sensory Funhouse, the kids enjoy trying to guess what certain objects are without being able to see them. Justin says, "You can touch everything. It's so much fun."

The Making of Me

Where do babies come from? That question and many more are answered in the film *The Making of Me*. The movie is shown in a theater in the middle of the Wonders of Life pavilion. It lasts 14 minutes. It's a good show to watch with your parents.

UNIVERSE OF ENERGY

Discover where energy comes from on this trip through prehistoric times, complete with dinosaurs. The ride is called Ellen's Energy Adventure. It's inside the Universe of Energy pavilion.

Ellen's energy nightmare

The attraction starts with a movie about a woman named Ellen. She is asleep and having a weird dream. She's a contestant on a TV game show—and all of the questions are about energy. Ellen doesn't know much about energy, so she really stinks at the game.

Then Bill Nye, the Science Guy decides to teach her all about energy. To do it, he takes her (and you) on a trip back in time.

Visit the dinosaurs

First you go into a theater to see another movie. Then the ride part begins. Bill Nye takes you and Ellen to a prehistoric world. You travel through fog and past several types of dinosaurs. Some of them are huge. And they all look real.

At the end of the ride, Ellen gets another chance to play on the TV game show. How does she do this time? That's something you'll have to see for yourself!

Three cheers for energy!

The kids who worked on this book loved Ellen's Energy Adventure. If you like dinosaurs, you'll enjoy it, too. Michael says, "It's an entertaining show. The movies talk about how energy got started, but it's a ride at the same time." Danielle T. thinks "it's neat how the cars split up in the theater. And the Audio-Animatronics dinosaurs and Ellen look real." Szasha says, "The dinosaur part is my favorite. And Ellen is funny."

World Showcase

Anyone can be a world traveler at World Showcase. You can learn about other countries, experience different cultures, and meet people from all over the world. Most of the people who work in each pavilion really come from the country they represent. And they're all happy to talk to you.

The 11 pavilions were built around a lake called World Showcase Lagoon. If you make the trip all the way around the lake, you will walk more than one mile!

CANADA

If you look at a map of our continent, Canada is at the top, just above the United States. It's a beautiful country. The Canada pavilion at Epcot is very pretty, too. There's a rocky mountain, a stream, gardens, and a totem pole.

The highlight is a movie called *O Canada!* The scenes completely surround you. Since you stand during the movie, it's easy to turn around and see everything.

What do the kids who worked on this book think about the movie? David explains, "It makes you feel like you're moving."

Ashley P. likes "the music and all the information the movie gives you about Canada."

Karyn says, "All the mountains and sledding scenes are beautiful." Nita agrees. "The movie is pretty," she says. "But I don't like standing up. They need seats in that theater!"

UNITED KINGDOM

From London to the English countryside, this pavilion gives a varied view of the United Kingdom. Some details to look for include the smoke stains painted on the chimneys to make them appear old, and the grassy roofs that are really made of plastic broom bristles. And Tate points out, "There are pretty gardens here."

Lindsay likes "looking at the different stores from the outside."

A group of comedians often performs along World Showcase Promenade near this pavilion. Sometimes, a band plays famous old songs in the garden.

FRANCE

The Eiffel Tower is the best-known landmark at the France pavilion. (The real one is in Paris, France.) The buildings here look just like those in a real French town. Many of the workers here come from France. They speak English with a French accent. Surprise them by saying *bonjour* (bohn-ZHOOR). It means "good day" in French.

The main attraction—besides the treats at the bakery—is *Impressions de France* (Impressions of France). It's a movie that takes you from one end of France to the other. It's shown on a big screen, and you get to sit down and take in the sights.

Just for Kids!

World Showcase has something special to offer kids: Kidcot Fun Stops. There's one in each country. They will give you the chance to make crafts and learn how kids have fun in different countries all over the world.

It's like a trip to France (almost)

"This movie makes me want to go to France," says Taran, "especially for the skiing." Anna says, "Now I'd like to go see all those places." Karyn has been to France, so it's interesting to her. She says, "It's more fun if you know what you're looking at."

Brad enjoys "the flying parts. It feels like you're really there." Brian L. thinks the "music is great, and I like the skiing and what they show of the country." Lindsay sums it up: "This movie is a great way to learn about France."

This is a nice place to take a break—the theater has comfy seats.

MOROCCO

The country of Morocco is famous for its mosaics—artwork and patterns that are made up of many tiles. That's why there is beautiful tile work in this pavilion. Moroccan artists made sure the mosaics here were done right.

The buildings are copies of monuments in Moroccan cities, including Fez and Marrakesh. There are lots of shops selling things you would find in Morocco. You can buy baskets, brass, jewelry, or a fez (a type of hat) and other Moroccan clothing.

The Marrakesh restaurant has a belly dancer who entertains in the courtyard, too.

Salam alekoum (sah-lahm wah-lay-koom) means "hello" in Morocco.

JAPAN

The temple out front, called a pagoda, makes the Japanese pavilion easy to spot. It's modeled after a pagoda in the city of Nara, Japan.

Be sure to notice all of the evergreen trees. In Japan, they are symbols of eternal life. Some of the trees found in a traditional Japanese garden will not survive in Florida. So similar trees were used instead.

Japanese drummers often perform outside the pavilion. The huge department store has lots of souvenirs from Japan.

Want to say "good morning" in Japanese? Just say *ohayo gozaimasu* (oh-hi-yoh goh-zy-ee-mahs).

THE AMERICAN ADVENTURE

This pavilion is the centerpiece of World Showcase. It's about the United States of America. That's why it's called The American Adventure.

The American Adventure show takes place inside Independence Hall (the real Independence Hall is in Philadelphia, Pennsylvania). The show celebrates the American spirit from the earliest days right up to the present.

Benjamin Franklin and Mark Twain host the show. They look so real, you may forget that they are mechanical. Ben Franklin even walks up stairs!

The American Adventure honors many heroes from history: the Pilgrims, Alexander Graham Bell,

Epcot

Jackie Robinson, Susan B. Anthony, Walt Disney, and more. Historic events are shown on movie screens.

Adam W. says, "The characters are so realistic. I like how they walk." Tate thinks the show is "very descriptive and very real." Justin wasn't sure at first if the characters were actors or Audio-Animatronics.

Anna thinks this show is "a perfect way to learn about our heritage. The best part is the movie that reviews many famous Americans."

ITALY

Venice is an Italian city known for waterways called canals. There are no canals at Epcot's Italy, but the pavilion does look a lot like the city. The tower is a smaller version of the Campanile, a famous building in Venice. Notice the gondolas tied to the dock in the lagoon. They are a type of boat used for traveling in the canals of Venice.

Tasty Italian chocolates and other goodies are for sale in the candy shop. The restaurant here is called Alfredo's. Inside, you can watch fresh pasta being made.

Say *buon giorno* (boo-on JOR-no). It means "good day" in Italian.

GERMANY

There isn't a village in Germany quite like the one at Epcot. It's a combination of cities and small towns from all around the country. Try to stop by on the hour so you can see the special clock and hear it chime.

Danielle G. says, "The buildings in Germany look authentic. In the center is a beautiful statue on top of a waterfall. I also like the cobblestone pavement." Tate suggests you "try the soft pretzels sold here. There's not much else to do, but it's cool to see how some buildings look in Germany."

In German, "good day" is *guten Tag* (GOOT-en tahkh).

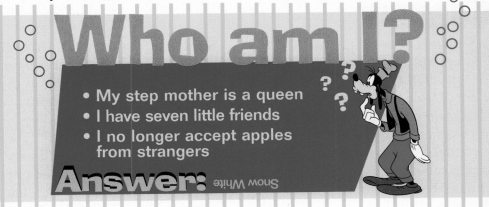

Who am I?

- My step mother is a queen
- I have seven little friends
- I no longer accept apples from strangers

Answer: Snow White

CHINA

Disney's version of the Temple of Heaven is at the center of this pavilion. It's a landmark in the Chinese city of Beijing. Inside, there is a Circle-Vision 360 movie called *Wonders of China: Land of Beauty, Land of Time*. (There are no seats in the theater.)

Before going in to see the movie, take a look at the waiting area. It's decorated in red and gold. These colors mean good luck in China.

The movie is beautiful, but it's a little long. It's more popular with adults than kids.

Karyn prefers the waiting area. "I think the movie is boring." But the exhibit is cool," she says.

To say "hello" in Chinese, say *ni hao* (nee HOW).

NORWAY

You will discover the history and culture of Norway at this pavilion. (Don't worry about the angry troll. He's harmless.)

The main building is a castle. It was based on an ancient fortress in the capital city of Oslo. Inside, there is a ride called Maelstrom. It's about Norway's history.

He has three heads!

The ride begins in a Viking village. (Vikings were explorers who lived about 1,000 years ago. Many came from Norway.) Next you travel to a forest, where a three-headed troll curses your boat and makes it go backward! After the boat trip, there is a short movie about Norway.

Short but sweet

How do kids feel about Maelstrom? Dawna says, "I like how we sit in a boat like the ones from Norway." David wishes the ride were longer. "I still think it's the best thing in World Showcase, even though it's so short."

Saying "hello" is easy here. It's *god dag* (goo DAHG).

HOT Go to Maelstrom late in the day, when the line is shorter. **TIP**

MEXICO

The pyramid-shaped building at the Mexico pavilion is home to El Río del Tiempo: The River of Time. This is a slow boat trip through scenes of Mexican life.

Film clips show cliff divers in Acapulco, speed boats in Manzanillo, and beautiful sea creatures in Isla Mujeres. You see many colorful displays showing Mexican traditions. At the end of the boat ride, you can visit several shops with Mexican crafts, sombreros, and colorful blankets.

Brad thinks "the boat ride is neat. There are so many things to look at." Dawna likes "the paintings, because I think Mexican art is really neat." Tate likes the way "the ride shows the beauty of the country."

"Hello" in Spanish is *hola* (OH-lah).

Entertainment

Epcot is known for its great entertainment. There are lots of shows and special performances every day of the year. For more information, check a park guidemap.

ILLUMINATIONS

An amazing fireworks show takes place each night on and around World Showcase Lagoon. It's called IllumiNations. You can see it from anywhere around the lagoon. (A new show will take its place in late 1999.)

JAMMITORS

One of the loudest shows is inside Future World, where musicians bang out rhythms on trash cans and, sometimes, on each other. Michael likes the Jammitors "because of the beats." Szasha says, "They're fun and funny. "

FOUNTAIN OF NATIONS

There is an enchanted fountain near Innoventions. It looks like a regular fountain, but it's not. Every 15 minutes, it performs a water ballet. The water moves to the music!

WORLD SHOWCASE PERFORMERS

There is some form of entertainment at each of the 11 pavilions in World Showcase. A couple of the highlights include The Living Statues in France and the British Invasion in the United Kingdom. The Living Statues are people dressed as statues. They look like they are made of stone, but then they surprise you by moving! The British Invasion is a funky band that sounds like The Beatles.

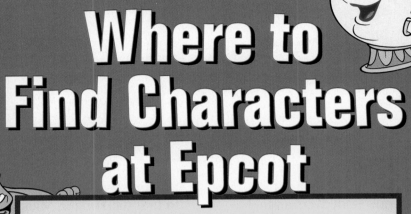

Where to Find Characters at Epcot

Mickey and his pals often appear at the **Centorium** shop. Sport Goofy can sometimes be spotted at the **Wonders of Life** pavilion. Dreamfinder and Figment sometimes drop by **Journey into Imagination**.

In World Showcase, you can greet Mickey and his closest friends at **The American Adventure**. You might find Belle and the Beast near **France**, Jasmine and Aladdin in **Morocco**, and Snow White in **Germany**. But the best spot for character sightings is the **United Kingdom**. Alice and the White Rabbit, Peter Pan and Captain Hook, Winnie the Pooh, and Mary Poppins all hang out here during the day. Check a park guidemap or ask a cast member for times.

EPCOT TIPS

Start your day early at Test Track. Then go to the Wonders of Life pavilion to ride Body Wars and see Cranium Command. If there's time before lunch, see Honey, I Shrunk the Audience at the Journey into Imagination pavilion.

Remember: World Showcase doesn't open until 11 A.M.

Need a refreshing splash? Visit the fountains by Journey into Imagination or the squirting sidewalk on the path to World Showcase.

Check the Tip Board in Innoventions Plaza. It lets you know how long the wait is for many attractions.

There is a special garbage can in the Electric Umbrella restaurant and a special drinking fountain near the Fountain of Nations. Why are they special? They talk!

Looking for a challenge? Try to find the Hidden Mickey at Spaceship Earth. (Hint: Look for it in the area where you get into the ride vehicles.)

Buy a passport at any World Showcase shop and get it stamped in every country. It's a great reminder of your trip.

Try not to see the movies at Canada, France, and China all in one day.

Take time to talk to the people who work in World Showcase. Most of them come from the country of the pavilion they represent, and they have many interesting stories to tell.

The area between Italy and The American Adventure is the best place to watch the fireworks show.

Attraction Ratings

COOL
(Check It Out)

- Journey into Imagination ride
- Food Rocks
- China
- Italy
- United Kingdom
- Mexico
- Germany
- Japan

REALLY COOL
(Don't Miss)

- The Living Seas
- The Circle of Life
- The American Adventure
- Spaceship Earth
- Mexico boat ride
- France
- Canada
- Morocco

THE COOLEST
(See at Least Twice)

- Test Track
- Body Wars
- Cranium Command
- Innoventions
- Universe of Energy
- Honey, I Shrunk the Audience
- Norway
- Living with the Land

Epcot

Your favorite Epcot attractions

Disney-MGM Studios

The Disney-MGM Studios lets you see some of the magic of making movies and TV shows. There are attractions that show how animation is done, how sound effects are made, how stunts are performed, and lots more.

The park looks a little like Hollywood did back in the 1940s. Hollywood is the California city where movie-making got its big start. The Disney-MGM Studios got its big start in 1989. It turns 10 years old this year. Don't forget to wish it happy birthday when you visit!

One of the best things about this park is that you can be a part of some attractions. It's fun to be right in the middle of the action, so be sure to volunteer. You'll also get to meet a ton of characters, including the stars of Disney's newest animated hit— so be sure to have your autograph book handy.

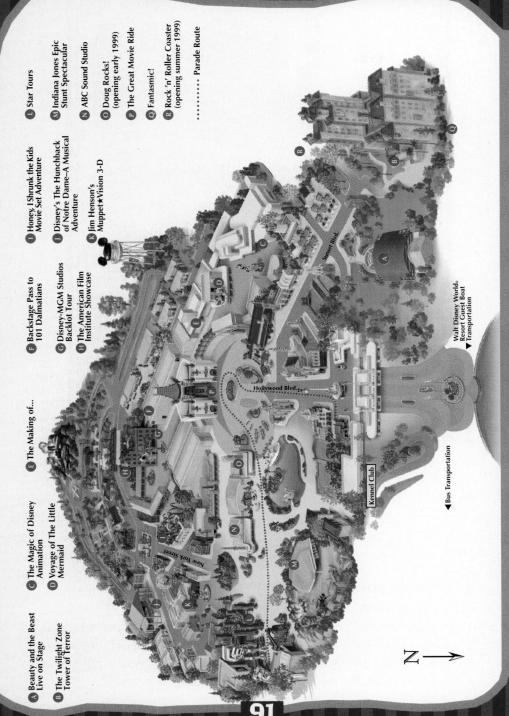

A Beauty and the Beast Live on Stage

B The Twilight Zone Tower of Terror

C The Magic of Disney Animation

D Voyage of The Little Mermaid

E The Making of...

F Backstage Pass to 101 Dalmatians

G Disney-MGM Studios Backlot Tour

H The American Film Institute Showcase

I Honey, I Shrunk the Kids Movie Set Adventure

J Disney's The Hunchback of Notre Dame–A Musical Adventure

K Jim Henson's Muppet★Vision 3-D

L Star Tours

M Indiana Jones Epic Stunt Spectacular

N ABC Sound Studio

O Doug Rocks! (opening early 1999)

P The Great Movie Ride

Q Fantasmic!

R Rock 'n' Roller Coaster (opening summer 1999)

·········· Parade Route

Hollywood Blvd.

Sunset Blvd.

New York Street

Kennel Club

▶ Walt Disney World® Resort Guest Boat Transportation

▶ Bus Transportation

N →

Use this map to explore the Disney-MGM Studios theme park.

The Twilight Zone Tower of Terror

Tower of Terror is the tallest attraction at Walt Disney World. For some people, it's also the scariest.

Legend says that one Halloween night, lightning hit The Hollywood Tower Hotel. A whole section of the hotel disappeared! So did an elevator carrying five people. No one ever saw them again.

Now the hotel is haunted. If you dare to enter it, you are in for a few surprises. First, you walk through the dusty hotel lobby. Then you enter a tiny room, where Rod Serling appears on TV. (He was the star of a sometimes scary show called "The Twilight Zone.") After Rod tells the story of The Hollywood Tower Hotel, get ready—you are on your way to the Twilight Zone.

Wait your turn

First, you have to wait in the boiler room of the hotel. And, as Dawna says, "Waiting just makes the suspense worse."

The ride takes you on a short tour of the hotel, where you see many special effects. Lindsay says, "I particularly like the ghosts of the people who disappeared."

The highlight comes when the elevator cables snap. Whoooosh! You plunge eight stories! Next the elevator shoots up to the hotel's 13th floor. It teeters for a moment and then . . . it drops to the ground at blazing speed!

Your picture is snapped in between drops. Chances are, you'll have a funny look on your face. Check out the photo as you exit the ride. (You don't have to buy the photo just to look at it.)

A thrilling experience

Kids agree that this is a great ride. Ashley J. says, "Waiting to fall is the scariest part." Lindsay says, "I was flying out of my seat!" She adds a warning: "Kids should know that about half the ride is in the dark."

You must be at least 40 inches tall to ride—and very brave!

Rock 'n' Roller Coaster

This ride really rocks! It travels at top speeds and flips you upside down three times. It also has a rock 'n' roll sound track that will have you dancing in your seat.

Scheduled to open in the summer of 1999, Rock 'n' Roller Coaster is Disney's fastest ride ever. It takes you from 0 to 60 miles per hour in the first three seconds of the ride! You need the speed because you're on your way to a party at a rock concert—and you're running late.

The ride takes place in a limousine on a roller coaster track. The track looks like a road in California. (You'll travel on the road to get to the concert hall.) The car radio is blasting, but you're not moving yet. Then, just as the concert starts, the light turns green and you're on your way. Hang on! You must be 44 inches tall to ride.

"I love all the costumes and the music."

Nita (age 14)

Beauty and the Beast Live on Stage

It's hard to keep quiet during this stage show—it makes you want to clap and sing along. The music comes straight from the Disney film *Beauty and the Beast.*

The story is the same, but the order of the songs is different. (A few songs are left out, too.)

Be their guest

The show starts with "Be Our Guest." It's a colorful musical number—just like in the movie. Then the show goes back to the beginning, where Belle is dreaming of faraway places. Soon, she is a prisoner in the Beast's castle. Lumière, Cogsworth, Mrs. Potts, and the rest of the gang are there to help. In the end, the spell is broken. The Beast becomes human again!

A real kid pleaser

Taran says, "If you love the movie, you'll like this show."

"I love when the white doves fly out at the end," says Nita. "I also love the costumes and the music." Karyn enjoys this show, too. "There are so many great details, like the dancing dishes and spoons," she says.

The show is performed several times each day. Read a park guidemap for exact times. (You can get a free map at any shop in the Disney-MGM Studios. Just ask!)

The sidewalk by The Great Movie Ride is covered with handprints. They belong to big Hollywood stars. Put your palms in the prints and compare your hands to theirs.

The Great Movie Ride

How many movies have you seen in your lifetime? Hundreds? Thousands? Well, how many have you actually been in? Probably not too many! This attraction lets you ride through scenes from old movies.

Pay attention!

First, you'll watch short clips from famous films. Pay close attention—these are the scenes that you will visit later on.

As you enter the ride vehicle, take time to look around. The room is set up like a movie set (a stage where movies are filmed). The background looks like the hills of Hollywood. That's the California town where movie-making got its big start.

A trip to Munchkinland

Once the car starts moving, you'll pass through scenes from movies like *Mary Poppins*, *Alien*, and *Fantasia*. One of the best scenes is straight out of the *Wizard of Oz*. It looks just like Munchkinland! (Beware: The Wicked Witch of the West pops in for a visit.)

You may also get caught in a shootout and come close to being slimed by an alien. The ride ends with a movie that shows more clips from great films.

What do kids think about The Great Movie Ride? "It's really cool," says Robert, "but it could have more action in it." Karyn disagrees. "No matter how many times I ride, I still love it."

The Magic of Disney Animation

Anybody can create a cartoon character. All you need is a pencil, some paper, and a little imagination. But how do you get that character to *move*? That's where the animation part comes in.

Learn how it's done

This attraction shows you how *Aladdin*, *The Lion King*, *Mulan*, and other movies were made. It also gives you a chance to watch artists working on a new Disney film, such as *Tarzan*.

In the waiting area, there are drawings on the walls. Later, you'll find out how artists called *animators* bring these kinds of sketches to life.

Spy on the animators

Toward the beginning of the tour, you get to meet a real Disney artist. There's even time for you to ask questions.

Later, you walk through a studio. It's where many animators work. (They are behind a glass wall, so you can see them.) To learn about what they are doing, just look at the TV screens overhead. A tour guide will explain the animation process.

It takes about 45 minutes to see everything. Try to go early in the day, when the animators are busy working. They usually go home at about 5 o'clock.

You Be the Animator

An animated character may have legs, but without a background, it has nothing to stand on! That's where the background animator comes to the rescue.

An artist has left Goofy up in the air. Draw a background so he doesn't float forever. Use your imagination to create the setting and mood for the scene.

Voyage of The Little Mermaid

You don't have to be a fish to have fun underwater—and this show proves it. In it, you go below the ocean's surface with Ariel and her friends from *The Little Mermaid*. They sing and act out the story on stage. Ariel and Eric are played by actors. Flounder, Sebastian, and other creatures are puppets.

Under the sea

There are some great special effects that draw you into the show. A screen of water makes it seem like the theater really is under the sea. Lasers flash, lightning strikes, and a mist sprays the audience. Scenes from the movie are shown on a big screen behind the stage.

A winning combination

Dawna thinks "the combination of actors, puppets, movie clips, lasers, bubbles, and water all add up to a great show."

"This is a totally creative show."

Lindsay
(age 9)

Lindsay agrees. "This is a totally creative show. You feel like you're under the water, especially when you get a little wet with the mist."

Tate thinks they leave out too much. "Even though most people know what happens, it would be better to have more scenes," he says.

Justin was surprised by the show. "I don't like *The Little Mermaid*," he says, "so I thought the show would be stupid. But it's really good."

HOT

For the best view at Voyage of The Little Mermaid, sit toward the back of the theater.

TIP

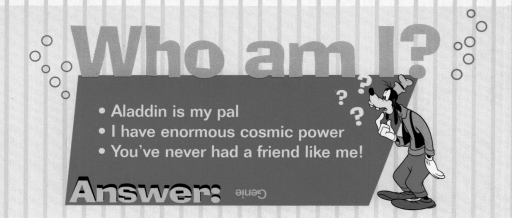

Who am I?

- Aladdin is my pal
- I have enormous cosmic power
- You've never had a friend like me!

Answer: Genie

Disney-MGM Studios

The Making of...

If you have ever wondered what goes into "the making of" a Disney movie, this attraction is for you. It goes behind the scenes and lets you in on many Hollywood secrets. You'll hear from directors, producers, and other people whose jobs are listed in movie credits.

The attraction changes every so often to keep up with the latest Disney films. Depending on when you go, you may see The Making of *Armageddon* or get a look at another live-action movie.

Sometimes the attraction is about kids' movies—sometimes it has more of an adult subject. Ashley J. thinks "probably grown-ups would like it more. If you are on a tight schedule, then maybe you shouldn't go to this one. But I learned a lot of things I didn't know about making movies."

HOT TIP

You can sing in the rain under a special umbrella on New York Street.

"I've never been on a tour that took me backstage like that."

Michael (age 11)

Backstage Pass to 101 Dalmatians

Puppies aren't very good actors. So how did movie-makers get hundreds of them to behave on the set of *101 Dalmatians*? They didn't. Most of the four-legged actors in the movie were fake. That's just one of the secrets you learn in this attraction. It shows how scenes from the live-action version of *101 Dalmatians* were filmed.

Tricks of the trade

Backstage Pass teaches you lots of movie-making tricks. You learn that film shot in front of a plain blue screen can be combined with almost any background. You also find out how sets are created, and may even see a new movie being filmed. The last part of the tour is about Cruella de Vil and the props and costumes that help make her seem so evil.

A different kind of tour

"I've never been on a tour that took me backstage like that," says Michael. "We got to see actual props from the movie."

Szasha thinks "knowing the story makes it more enjoyable." But Dan hasn't seen the movie and likes this tour. "It's still interesting," he says. "Some of the things look so real and they are fake. The horse that kicked Cruella in the face is really a robot."

Disney-MGM Studios

Disney-MGM Studios Backlot Tour

There's a real working studio at this theme park. A tram ride lets you see parts of the backstage areas where movies and TV shows are filmed. You also see how a battle scene at sea is shot.

A grand canyon

The trip includes a stop at Catastrophe Canyon—a special effects area. Here you see a fire and a flash flood. The tram also takes you through the costume and lighting departments, and past props from famous movies.

"I like Catastrophe Canyon," says Lissy. "It shows that special effects are safer than they look."

Robert agrees. "Catastrophe Canyon is really cool. When the explosions go off, it gets really hot. Then when the water comes down, it gets really cold."

Where's the back door?

Ashley P. enjoys touring the streets and "seeing the houses without the backs. They only film the fronts for the television shows, so that's all they build," she points out.

Nita has seen this attraction before. "I like this tour," she says, "but a lot depends on the guide. If you get a really good guide, the tour is much better."

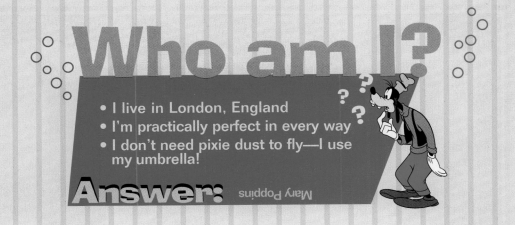

Who am I?

- I live in London, England
- I'm practically perfect in every way
- I don't need pixie dust to fly—I use my umbrella!

Answer: Mary Poppins

Honey, I Shrunk the Kids Movie Set Adventure

The backyard from the *Honey, I Shrunk the Kids* movie has been re-created as a big playground. Even grown-ups feel small here. There are 30-foot blades of grass, huge Lego toys, a giant ant, and more. There are things to climb on, slide down, and explore.

"It looks more like *Honey, I Blew Up the Garden*!" says Taran. "I like the cave the best."

Lissy thinks "the whole place is really neat. Not just the slides and the swings—there's a lot for older kids to notice. Everything looks like it comes straight from the movie."

Most kids enjoy getting wet under the leaky hose. Water squirts from a different spot each time.

"I like the slides and the big net, but I think it's more for younger kids," says Brian L.

Karyn agrees. "I'm the type of person who would just love to take a younger kid around and watch them have fun."

HOT TIP! There's a big map at the entrance to Honey, I Shrunk the Kids Movie Set Adventure. Use it!

Jim Henson's Muppet*Vision 3-D

Don't miss this attraction—it's one of Walt Disney World's best. It begins with a funny pre-show starring Fozzie Bear, Gonzo, Scooter, and Sam Eagle. Then you go into a special theater that looks just like the one from the old "Muppet Show." Here, you see 3-D movie effects mixed with some other special effects. It's hard to tell what's part of the movie and what's real.

Amazing effects

"The characters come right out at you," says Lissy. "It's cool that they have real things happening, so when they throw a pie you think it will be real." Adam W. enjoys the show. "My favorite parts are the squirting water and when the screen blows up. You feel like you're going to get hit."

Kirsti is a Muppet fan, too. "This is my favorite show and it always will be, " she says. Taran thinks "it's

awesome. I also love the little 3-D character, Waldo, because he seems like he's talking only to you." (Waldo isn't really a Muppet. He's a special character that was dreamed up just for this show.)

Everybody loves Waldo

Robert and Anna feel the same way. "I thought Waldo was pointing just at me. I can't believe he was pointing at everyone," says Robert.

And Anna says, "Waldo looks like he's right in front of you."

Look around the theater

Nita says to look at the back of the theater "because a lot happens back there and most people miss it."

Karyn says, "You have to see this movie a few times to get all the jokes and appreciate more of the details, like the two guys sitting in the balcony. They're really funny."

Star Tours

Soar through the galaxy on an out-of-control spaceship and experience the thrills of the movie *Star Wars*. Your pilot is Captain Rex. He's new on the job and can't seem to find his way through all the giant ice crystals and other spaceships.

It feels real

This ride takes place on a flight simulator, the same type used to train astronauts and pilots. The combination of the simulator and the movie makes you feel like you're really rocketing through outer space.

Rex is a rotten pilot

Brad says, "The pilot makes the ride really fun. He keeps going the wrong way." Robert thinks "it's really neat. It's funny when the pilot can't find the brakes. If you know

Get a Taste of Toy Story

The **Toy Story Pizza Planet Arcade** looks like the restaurant in the movie. Located near Jim Henson's Muppet*Vision 3-D, this arcade has video games, plus a fast-food counter with pizza, pasta salad, and juice boxes. Brian F. says, "I like it because it's just like the movie."

Ashley J. Points out that, in the middle of the room, there's a life-size model of the game with "all the little aliens from Toy Story." She says, "It would be better if it were real."

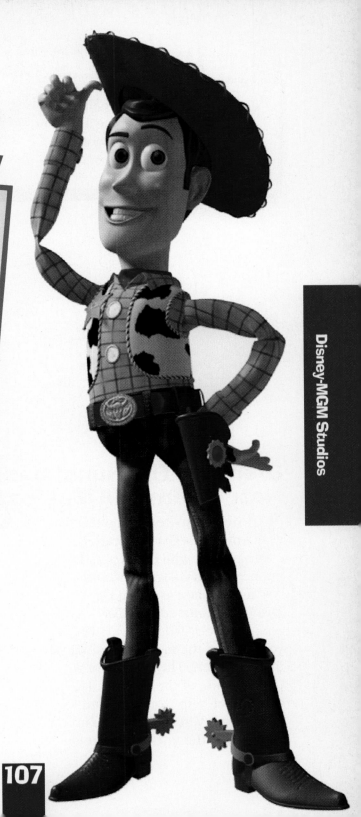

what the movie *Star Wars* is like, you'll really like this ride."

Danielle G. agrees. "It feels and looks like you're really traveling through space." Dawna adds, "It seems like you're going really fast even though you're not going anywhere."

You must be at least 40 inches tall to ride.

Coming Attraction

A brand-new attraction will open at the Disney-MGM Studios this year. If you're a fan of the 12-year-old animated star Doug, then you'll love this show. It's all about him! Of course, his faithful pup Porkchop will be by his side for this all-new adventure at 21 Jumbo Street.

Disney's The Hunchback of Notre Dame—A Musical Adventure

You are invited to the Festival of Fools. The celebration is packed with dancers and puppets, all in colorful costumes.

This live show is based on Disney's animated film *The Hunchback of Notre Dame*. If you've seen the movie, you'll know the characters. The storyteller is Clopin, King of the Gypsies. He gets lots of help from his band of gypsy players, who sing, dance, and act out the tale. Judge Frollo, Esmeralda, and Phoebus also make appearances. And those wacky gargoyles, Victor, Hugo, and Laverne are there to make everybody laugh.

Szasha says, "I think it's a cool play, even though I haven't seen the movie. I like the puppets and live actors. Quasimodo rings the bells by pulling a rope, and they really work." Danielle T. likes "how the actors go into the audience. Their costumes are great."

Indiana Jones Epic Stunt Spectacular

Fire, explosions, daring escapes, and other special effects are the stars of this attraction. Stunt men and women act out scenes from the movie *Raiders of the Lost Ark* and show how special effects are done. The audience watches from a large theater, and several adults are chosen to perform with the pros. (It's too dangerous for kids.)

Fun for everyone

"I love this show. I think it's great for all ages," says Karyn. One of the best parts of the show is the scene where the giant ball rolls down and seems to crush Indiana Jones. "I was at the edge of my seat!" says Brian L.

Don't try this at home

Lissy says the music adds to the suspense and "the stunt people are just fantastic." Brian L. views it as pure excitement: "I love how they were falling from the towers, and then they were always okay."

You learn a lot about movie stunts at this show. "They explain everything they do, making it even more fun to watch," says Karyn.

"We got to do voices, clattering, clopping—everything!"

Seth (age 10)

ABC Sound Studio

Here you can see how they make the sounds for movies and cartoons—and how hard it is to get them just right. Members of the audience are chosen to make sound effects for a film or short cartoon.

Everybody makes sounds

Usually, the volunteers don't do a very good job. Sounds end up in all the wrong places! But that's all part of the fun. (The rest of the audience gets to make noises, too.) Most kids enjoy this attraction—especially when they get to volunteer.

Mess-ups can be funny

Lindsay thinks "it's great to see how some of the sounds are made. There are a lot of mess-ups, and that's really funny."

Seth got picked to go on stage. "We got to do voices, clattering, clopping—everything!" he says.

After the show, visit the area called SoundWorks for some do-it-yourself sound effects. It's by the exit of the ABC Sound Studio. "The 3-D room is really fun," says Tate. "Everything sounds like it's really happening to you."

Autographs

Entertainment

Lights! Camera! Action! There's a lot of star-studded entertainment at the Disney-MGM Studios. Most of it has a TV or movie theme. Two of the best shows are described below.

MULAN PARADE

The star of *Mulan* marches in a parade on Hollywood Boulevard every afternoon. Look for fancy floats, brave soldiers, and giant puppets, plus the Matchmaker, Shang, and Mulan's trusty sidekick, Mushu.

Shan Yu, the villain from the movie, is here, too. But don't expect him to join the celebration—he's all tied up on a bed of skulls.

FANTASMIC!

What does Mickey Mouse dream about? You can find out at Fantasmic! It's an amazing show that combines fireworks, Disney characters, music, and a little magic.

Mickey's dreams are fun to watch—but some of them are a little scary. (Disney villains keep turning his dreams into nightmares.) In the end, good wins over evil and Mickey's dreams are happy once more.

The show is presented in the Hollywood Hills Amphitheater behind The Twilight Zone Tower of Terror attraction.

Where to Find Characters at Disney-MGM Studios

There are lots of places to meet Disney characters at the Studios. One of the best spots is just outside The Magic of Disney Animation attraction. It's called **Animation Courtyard**. Disney characters stop by all day. Go late in the afternoon when there aren't as many people, and you can get a ton of pictures. If you check a park guidemap or ask a cast member, you can find the times that characters are scheduled to appear.

Characters also greet guests on **Mickey Avenue** and **New York Street**. But don't go looking for Mickey Mouse on Mickey Avenue. He sticks to **Sunset Boulevard**. If you want to meet Buzz and Woody, head for Mickey Avenue.

DISNEY-MGM STUDIOS TIPS

Arrive at the Disney-MGM Studios before the opening time. The gates usually open about a half hour before the scheduled time.

The character breakfast at the Soundstage restaurant is a great way to start the day.

There is one "chicken exit" at Tower of Terror, right before you get on the ride elevator, just in case you change your mind at the last minute.

Check the Tip Board on Hollywood Boulevard. It tells you which attractions have the shortest lines and when the next shows start.

Some stage shows don't open until late morning. Be sure to check your guidemap for exact showtimes.

To get a good spot to see the afternoon parade, line up on Hollywood Boulevard about 30 minutes early.

Animation Courtyard is the best place to meet Disney characters.

Tower of Terror has very long lines. See it early in the day but never right after a meal.

See Muppet*Vision 3-D, Voyage of The Little Mermaid, and Star Tours in the morning before the lines get too long.

Attraction Ratings

COOL
(Check It Out)

- The Great Movie Ride
- Backstage Pass to 101 Dalmatians
- The Hunchback of Notre Dame show
- The Making of...

REALLY COOL
(Don't Miss)

- Indiana Jones Epic Stunt Spectacular
- ABC Sound Studio
- Disney-MGM Studios Backlot Tour
- Honey, I Shrunk the Kids Movie Set Adventure

THE COOLEST
(See at Least Twice)

- Jim Henson's Muppet*Vision 3-D
- Star Tours
- Tower of Terror
- Beauty and the Beast Live on Stage
- The Magic of Disney Animation
- Voyage of The Little Mermaid

Your favorite Disney-MGM Studios attractions

Disney's Animal Kingdom

The newest park in Walt Disney World is called Animal Kingdom. It celebrates animals of every kind, from lions, tigers, and zebras to alligators that lived during the time of the dinosaurs. And they're all real! You may get closer to them than you've ever been before. There are dinosaurs, too. The dinos aren't real, but they sure seem it.

Animal Kingdom is a huge theme park with many attractions. Five Magic Kingdoms could fit inside it. Just like at the Magic Kingdom, there are different "lands" to visit in Animal Kingdom. The major lands are Safari Village, DinoLand U.S.A., Asia, Africa, and Camp Minnie-Mickey.

You enter the park through The Oasis. It's a big garden with plants and animals. Take some time to look around. Then cross a bridge to Safari Village and decide which land to explore first.

SAFARI VILLAGE

A The Tree of Life

B The Tree of Life Garden

C It's Tough to be a Bug!

D Discovery River Boats
at Safari Village

CAMP MINNIE-MICKEY

E Festival of the Lion King

F Colors of the Wind; Friends
from the Animal Forest at
Grandmother Willow's Grove

DINOLAND U.S.A.

G Countdown to Extinction

H The Boneyard

I Cretaceous Trail

J Journey into Jungle Book
at Theater in the Wild

AFRICA

K Kilimanjaro Safaris

L Gorilla Falls
Exploration Trail

M Wildlife Express
to Conservation Station

N Conservation Station

ASIA

O Discovery River Boats
at Upcountry Landing

P Flights of Wonder
at Caravan Stage

Q Maharajah Jungle Trek

R Tiger Rapids Run
(opening spring 1999)

CONSERVATION STATION
Take the Wildlife Express from Harambe
in Africa to explore Conservation Station

What's the best way to see Animal Kingdom? Use this map to help you decide!

Safari Village

Safari Village is the island gateway to all the other lands in the park. The Tree of Life stands near the center of Safari Village. If you wander about its roots you'll see all kinds of animals.

The Tree of Life

This man-made tree is 145 feet tall. From far away it looks like any other tree. When you get up close, you'll realize that this is not an ordinary tree. It's covered with animals!

Artists have carved 325 animal images into its trunk. In fact, it's called The Tree of Life because it's covered with so many different kinds of animal life.

Michael thinks "The Tree of Life is great because you can see the animals carved into it." Danielle T. agrees. "I could probably stare at The Tree of Life all day and still not see all of the carvings," she says. How many can *you* spot?

❝The Tree of Life is great because you can see all the animals carved into it.❞

Michael (age 11)

It's Tough to be a Bug!

The Tree of Life has a hollow trunk. It's cool, dark, and roomy inside. That makes it a great place to watch a 3-D movie called It's Tough to be a Bug! It's hosted by Flik, the star of *A Bug's Life*.

This movie is about the tiny creatures that outnumber all others on our planet—bugs. In it, animated insects use music and special effects to show how hard their lives are. It's a very funny show (and a little bit scary).

Discovery River Boats

Like all islands, Safari Village is surrounded by water. In this case, the waterway is called Discovery River. You can board a boat in Safari Village (or Asia) and take a tour on the river.

Along the way, you'll discover surprises, including a water dinosaur and a fire-breathing dragon (the dragon is in a cave).

HOT TIP

If you hate creepy crawlers, skip It's Tough to be a Bug!

There are surprises *inside* the boat, too. Creepy critters like skunks and tarantulas often come along for the ride. An expert can answer your questions about them.

If you don't mind the creatures on board, this ride can be very relaxing. Michael says to "do it first so you can see the lands before you visit them."

DinoLand

The entrance to this land is marked by a giant dinosaur skeleton. Inside, you will find life-like dinosaurs as well as live animals that have existed since prehistoric times. The main attraction is Countdown to Extinction, but there are lots of other things to see and do. You can dig for bones in an amazing playground or explore a nature trail. When you're ready to slow down a bit, stop and see Journey into Jungle Book at Theater in the Wild, or get a bite to eat at Restaurantosaurus.

Countdown to Extinction

This thrilling ride takes you back to the last few minutes of the Cretaceous Period. (That's when the dinosaurs died out.)

Save the dinosaur

At Countdown to Extinction, your job is to save the last iguanodon. You have to brave a meteor shower and the largest Audio-Animatronics creature Disney has ever made. It's a dinosaur called a carnotaurus, and it may be the ugliest thing you've ever seen. This monster has the face of a toad, horns like a bull, and squirrel-like arms. It looks like it's alive. The nostrils even move as it breathes. And, boy, can it run. The carnotaurus runs for about 30 feet. Be careful! This hungry monster is not just after the iguanodon—it wants to eat *you*, too.

An exciting (and scary) ride

The kids agree that this is a very exciting ride, but one that might not be for everyone. "Countdown to Extinction is really cool," says Dan. "I don't know if my brother would want to ride it, though. He's

120

U.S.A.

"If you get nightmares, Countdown to Extinction might not be a good idea."

Danielle T. (age 12)

7 and he might get scared."
Danielle T. has a tip: "If
you get nightmares,
Countdown to
Extinction might not
be a good idea."
Szasha's not

taking any chances. "The
dinosaur ride sounds
scary," she says. "I don't
like scary rides."

You must be 48 inches
tall to ride.

Cretaceous Trail

For a real "live" treat, walk down the Cretaceous Trail. This short path is filled with plants and animals that have been around longer than people have. Their ancestors lived with dinosaurs! Be on the lookout for birds and alligators and other ancient beasts.

The trail is a peaceful way to pass some time after riding Countdown to Extinction—or if you are waiting while others ride.

The Boneyard

Are you ready to dive into the biggest sand box you've ever seen? It's here and it's filled with bones! You can uncover the bones of a mammoth and find clues about how the animal died.

There are also dinosaur footprints that roar when you jump in them, and a xylophone that's made of dinosaur bones. There's a rope maze for climbing and plenty of slippery slides, too. Be sure to check out the OldenGate Bridge.

It's made from a huge dinosaur skeleton.

"This place is amazing," says Robbie. "I dug up an entire part of a bone." The Boneyard can be a lot of fun, but it's not for everyone. Amy thinks "sandboxes are pretty babyish." But she did make one exciting discovery: a Hidden Mickey! See if you can find it when you visit. (Hint: It's near the digging area.)

HOT TIP

The xylophone is next to the truck in The Boneyard. Press the bones to make music.

Journey into Jungle Book

If you like *The Jungle Book*, this show is a bare necessity! Mowgli, Baloo, and other characters from the film are here. Together they dance their way through jungle adventures at the Theater in the Wild. They also sing songs from the movie, including "The Bare Necessities" and "I Wanna Be Like You."

Mowgli is in danger

Kids enjoy this show, but it helps to know what the story is about before you go. In case you haven't seen *The Jungle Book*, it's about a young boy named Mowgli. (His animal friends call him a man cub.) He grew up in the jungle.

Mowgli is happy in his home, but his friends are afraid for his safety. Shere Khan, the tiger, is heading Mowgli's way. And he doesn't like humans one bit.

A wise panther named Bagheera wants to protect the boy. He takes him on a journey to a "man village." Along the way, they meet up with the fun-loving bear Baloo, the slithery snake Kaa, and lots of other jungle beasts.

Hold that tiger

How is the show better than the movie? The kids say it's the sets. "The scenes are really cool," Robbie says, "and the tiger is awesome."

Africa

Before creating this land, Disney Imagineers spent months on the continent of Africa learning all about the plants and animals there. When they came back, they made an African forest and a grassland in Florida. Then they filled it with hundreds of the same animals they had seen in Africa. Most of the animals in Animal Kingdom came from special parks and zoos around the world. You can see many animals on a safari ride and learn about them at Conservation Station.

Kilimanjaro Safaris

In this wild jungle adventure, you ride in a vehicle that's wide open. There's almost nothing between you and the animals! You see zebras, lions, cheetahs, rhinos, elephants, and more. Some animals may even come up close. But don't worry—the dangerous animals can't get near you.

After a calm sight-seeing tour, the ride takes a different twist. There are poachers hunting for elephants, and the animals need your help. You begin a wild chase over muddy roads. Do you catch the bad guys? You will have to go on the ride to find out!

Kids love the Kilimanjaro Safaris. Amy thought it was a super ride, although she wished there were even more animals to see. Seth says, "If you like adventure, but don't like to be scared, this ride is for you."

❝Seeing the gorillas up close is amazing.❞

Szasha (age 8)

Gorilla Falls Exploration Trail

After you take a ride on the Kilimanjaro Safaris, go for a walk on the Gorilla Falls Exploration Trail. This nature trail is filled with many exciting sights. You'll come nose-to-nose with a naked mole rat and look for hippos underwater. Exotic fish and birds live in the African Aviary.

No binoculars necessary

Pick up a bird guide (they should be hanging on a post in the aviary) and see how many different birds you can spot. Afterward, make a stop at the meerkat exhibit. Some people call it the "Timon exhibit" because he's a meerkat. (There are no Pumbaas here, though. Meerkats and warthogs don't get along in real life.)

Greetings, gorillas

Toward the end of the trail, you may have the chance to come face-to-face with gorillas. Szasha thinks this is the perfect place to visit after the safari ride. "Seeing the gorillas up close is amazing," she says.

Disney's Animal Kingdom

Who am I?

- I smell
- Grubs are my favorite snack
- My best buddy is a meerkat

Answer: Pumbaa

Wildlife Express to Conservation Station

There's only one way to get to Conservation Station: by train. Along the way, it takes you on a behind-the-scenes tour of the buildings where animals are cared for. It also shows where the elephants and rhinos stay at night. You can hop aboard the Wildlife Express in Africa. When you're done exploring Conservation Station, jump back on the train. It will take you back to civilization.

Conservation Station

There's more to Animal Kingdom than watching wild creatures. It's also a place to learn about what animals need to survive—and what people can do to help. You can do that at Conservation Station.

This is where a team of doctors, scientists, and animal keepers work to make sure the animals in the park get everything they need. There is an animal hospital, places for baby animals to sleep and get special care, and lots of shows meant to get you excited about conservation. There are even ways to find out about conservation projects near your home.

Talk to the animals

Many of the exhibits are interactive. In Song of the Rain Forest, you're surrounded by the sounds you might hear in a real rain forest. At the Look-in Lab, you can watch veterinarians care for baby animals. People can walk among animals like goats and sheep in the Affection Section. Go ahead and pet them, but remember: There's no feeding allowed.

66**I'm glad there's a conservation area so we can learn to save the animals.**99

Danielle T. (age 12)

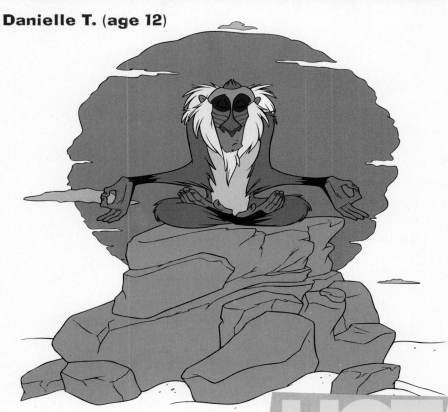

Kids care

The kids feel that Conservation Station is an important part of the park. They think everyone should help care for the world's animals and the environment.

"I'm glad there's a conservation area so we can learn to save the animals," Danielle T. says. Szasha agrees. "If we don't help them, they could become extinct," she adds.

HOT TIP

Conservation Station is a great place to stay dry when it rains.

Asia

Asia is the largest continent on earth. It's almost twice as big as North America! Asia is also the name of the newest land in Animal Kingdom. It's a lot smaller than the real thing, but it gives you an idea of what the Asian continent is like. It has jungles and rain forests and magnificent animals. It's also home to the fastest raging river in Walt Disney World—Tiger Rapids. If you're feeling brave, you can shoot the rapids on a wild thrill ride. For a calmer experience, head for the Caravan Stage.

Maharajah Jungle Trek

Put on your walking shoes and keep your eyes peeled. This jungle trail is the place to spot tigers, deer, antelope, gibbons (small apes that live in trees), and strange, scaly animals called Komodo dragons. You'll also see many colorful birds along the way and tons of plants and trees. After all, it is a jungle.

In the middle of the jungle is the Bat Pavilion. Giant bats live here. Their wings are enormous! In some places, there's no glass between you and the bats. But don't worry— they're not interested in humans.

HOT TIP

There is no roof at Flights of Wonder. Wear sunscreen!

Tiger Rapids Run

This is one of the wettest and wildest rides in Walt Disney World. (It is scheduled to open in the spring of 1999.) The ride begins as a peaceful raft trip through a rain forest. But things don't stay calm for very long.

You will soon see how logging (cutting down trees for lumber) can destroy the rain forest. One of the saddest sights is a section of forest that's been burned down. Up ahead, there's a fire raging out of control. Blazing logs block the river, and your raft heads right for them!

What happens next? We won't tell. (Fear not—there's a happy ending. This is Walt Disney World, after all.) You must be at least 46 inches tall to ride.

Flights of Wonder

Live birds are the stars of this show that takes place on the Caravan Stage. They swoop and soar and do amazing tricks.

One of the best performers is Groucho the parrot. He can't wait to entertain you. What is his special talent? He can sing! One of his favorite tunes is "How Much Is that Doggie in the Window?" Do you know that song?

Disney's Animal Kingdom

Camp Minnie-

Disney characters have their very own vacation spot right here in Animal Kingdom. It's called Camp Minnie-Mickey and it's a great place to meet Mickey, Minnie, Goofy, Pooh, Tigger, King Louie, Rafiki, and their friends. To find your favorite characters, just follow the trails through the forest. But save time to see the two shows while you're here.

Colors of the Wind, Friends from the Animal Forest

Who can save the forest? The wise old tree, Grandmother Willow, knows the answer. But she won't tell. She wants Pocahontas to figure it out for herself.

This show is performed at Grandmother Willow's Grove. It takes you and Pocahontas on a journey through the forest. Together, you'll meet many different animals: an armadillo, a hawk, a skunk, even a boa constrictor. And they are all real! During the show, you will learn that every animal has its own special talent. You'll also discover which animal can stop the forest from being destroyed.

Festival of the Lion King

This is one spectacular musical show. Even if you have the movie memorized, you're in for a few surprises. All of the major characters from the movie are here, but they look a little different. Most of them are played by humans dressed in African costumes.

An action-packed performance

The theater has big stages that look like parade floats. (That's because they were once used in a parade at Disneyland!) On one, Simba sits atop Pride Rock. The wisecracking Pumbaa sits on another. Monkeys use the center stage as a trampoline. They jump and do tricks in the air.

Kids love the festival

"This show is really neat," says Seth. "It's a trapeze act and ballet with a Disney twist." Robbie likes it, too. "The dancers are full of energy," he says. And Amy thinks "the costumes and dances are great." Kirsti loved the show, but warns: "The music is a little loud."

This is a very popular show. Check a park guidemap for times and arrive at least 30 minutes before it starts.

Disney's Animal Kingdom

Entertainment

Everyone loves a parade, so of course there's one in Animal Kingdom. There are also street musicians, storytellers, live animals, and many other things to entertain you. Read all about them below.

AFRICAN ENTERTAINMENT

African music fills the air in the village of Harambe. Live bands perform here throughout the day.

ANIMAL ENCOUNTERS

Get to know our smaller animal friends as they roam through the park with their human keepers.

DINOLAND U.S.A. ENTERTAINMENT

A bunch of wacky performers is on the loose—and they will do anything to make you dig them! They usually drive around the area in a car, stopping to make noise along the way.

MARCH OF THE ANIMALS

In this parade, marchers wear colorful animal costumes as they dance through Safari Village. Look for creatures big and small, from tigers to termites.

SAFARI VILLAGE ENTERTAINMENT

Gather around as storytellers tell animal tales, while music based on sounds of nature plays in the background. This is also where wooden statues surprise visitors by coming to life.

Where to Find Characters at Animal Kingdom

It's easy to find Disney characters at Animal Kingdom—they have a land all their own. **Camp Minnie-Mickey** is the best place to meet characters in this park.

There are four little huts toward the back of Camp Minnie-Mickey. Different characters hang out at them all day. Just follow one of the paths (and stand in line) to meet Mickey, Goofy, Timon, Winnie the Pooh, Tigger, and other Disney favorites. Don't forget your autograph book (you can use page 111 of this book for autographs). Donald Duck, Pluto, and other characters host breakfast at **Restaurantosaurus**.

ANIMAL KINGDOM TIPS

Try to arrive very early. The park may open as early as 7:30 A.M. This is Walt Disney World's newest theme park, so it will probably be really busy in the middle of the day.

Go to the thrill rides—Countdown to Extinction and Tiger Rapids Run—early, before they get too crowded.

On the Kilimanjaro Safaris ride, look at the back of the seat in front of you. The pictures will show you which animals you're about to see.

The animals are more active in the morning.

Check the Tip Boards in Safari Village to find out how long the wait is for the most popular attractions.

It's Tough to be a Bug! (inside The Tree of Life) is **very scary** to some kids. In it, bugs shoot quills, spiders fall from above, and creepy critters scamper beneath your seat.

It's fun to see how many animals you can find carved into The Tree of Life and the other buildings in Safari Village.

Look for your favorite Disney characters in Camp Minnie-Mickey. It's the best place to find them in the park.

Save time for all of the hands-on exhibits in Conservation Station.

Check out the thunder and lightning effects inside the Rainforest Cafe.

Attraction Ratings

COOL
(Check It Out)

- The Oasis
- Discovery River Boats
- Flights of Wonder
- Cretaceous Trail

REALLY COOL
(Don't Miss)

- Journey into Jungle Book
- The Boneyard
- Gorilla Falls Exploration Trail
- Maharajah Jungle Trek
- Colors of the Wind, Friends from the Animal Forest

THE COOLEST
(See at Least Twice)

- Kilimanjaro Safaris
- Tiger Rapids Run
- Festival of the Lion King
- Countdown to Extinction
- It's Tough to be a Bug!

Your favorite Animal Kingdom attractions

Everything Else in the World

No matter what you're interested in—water fun, sports, or animals—Walt Disney World has enough to make every minute of your vacation a blast. After you visit the theme parks, there's still so much to do. There are three water parks, speedy boats to rent, an island where animals are cared for, and lots of neat shopping spots.

If you're into sports, check out Disney's Wide World of Sports complex, rent a bike, or test your skills at miniature golf. For a peek at some Disney secrets, take a behind-the-scenes tour.

In this chapter, you can read up on all the extra activities and find out about hotels and restaurants at Walt Disney World. Then you can help your family decide where to stay, where to eat, and what to do when you're not at the theme parks.

Character Confusion!

Walt Disney World is crawling with characters. They sing. They dance. They've even been known to sign autographs for fans like you! Some of those characters are listed below. How many of their names can you unscramble? Use a pen (and your brain) to match the unscrambled names on the right with the scrambled ones on the left.

1. yodow	A. Frollo
2. foyog	B. Skuttle
3. alobo	C. Ursula
4. bamis	D. Mulan
5. alurus	E. Goofy
6. tutslek	F. Baloo
7. noldrefu	G. Lumiere
8. loflor	H. Woody
9. reemuli	I. Flounder
10. lamun	J. Simba

ANSWERS: 1.H,2.E,3.F,4.J,5.C,6.B,7.I,8.A,9.G,10.D

Waters of

It's easy to get wet, stay cool, and have fun at Walt Disney World. That's because it's a water wonderland. Choose from three water parks or take a dip in your hotel pool. If you're under the age of 10, you must bring a grown-up with you to the water parks.

Typhoon Lagoon

A typhoon is a powerful, windy storm. It dumps huge amounts of rain and sends objects flying through the air. This water park looks like a typhoon hit it. There's even a boat stuck on a mountain top! Of course, a storm didn't really put the boat there—Disney Imagineers did. They also put in pools, water slides, and a raft ride.

Catch a wave

The biggest pool here is like a small ocean. It has 4½-foot waves. That makes body-surfing fun. There are also two speed slides to try. They send you zipping through a dark cave. For a calmer ride, you can slip into a tube and float along a river. Afterward, you can glide down more water slides.

There's also a special area just for younger kids—Ketchakiddee Creek. It has small slides and other games.

Swim with the sharks

Shark Reef is an amazing part of Typhoon Lagoon. It's the home of nurse sharks, bonnethead sharks, and leopard sharks. And you can splash around with them. Don't worry—these sharks are friendly. They don't mind when people swim in their tank. Are you brave enough to swim with the sharks? (You must be at least 10 years old.)

Blizzard Beach

Would you wear a bathing suit to a snow-covered mountain? Probably not. But you should wear one to Blizzard Beach. It looks like a place to ski, but it's really a water park. So don't worry if you can't ski. Nobody skis down the mountain here. They slide!

Mountain climbing

Like a real ski resort, all the action centers around a mountain. In this case, it's Mount Gushmore. To get to the top, you have to take a chair lift. The ride gives you a fantastic view of the whole park.

The scariest slide on the mountain is Summit Plummet. It begins 120 feet in the air, on a platform that looks like a ski jump. It drops you down a steep slide at about 60 miles per hour. That's faster than many cars go on the highway.

Slip-sliding away

There are plenty of other ways to slide down the mountain. Tube slides, body slides, and inner-tube rides can keep you busy all day long. It's fun to body-surf in the wave pool, too.

For preteens, there's Ski Patrol Training Camp, with its "iceberg" obstacle course, and ropes for swinging into the water. Tike's Peak is a special place for younger kids. It has slides and a snow-castle fountain play area.

As Karyn says, "This is one awesome water park."

Everything Else in the World

HOT TIP

Bring water shoes to the water parks. The ground gets hot— and so do your feet!

River Country

This may be the smallest Disney water park, but you can still have big fun here. You can zip down water slides, shoot the rapids in a tube, and swing from a rope and then drop into the lake. *Kerplunk!*

Disney Imagineers got the idea for River Country from books by Mark Twain: *The Adventures of Tom Sawyer* and *The Adventures of Huckleberry Finn*. In both stories, the boys splash in their favorite swimming spot.

Tom and Huck don't visit River Country—but other characters sometimes do. Goofy, Chip, and Dale are here to celebrate the Fourth of July all summer long. You can meet them, play tug-of-war, and join in potato sack races during the All-American Water Party. You might even get picked to be in a special parade!

To find out when the party is happening, have a parent call 407-824-2760.

Let's Get Wet!

Many other places around Walt Disney World offer chances to get wet. At the Magic Kingdom, head for Splash Mountain and sit in the front row. Or hang around Donald's Boat at Mickey's Toontown Fair. Ariel's Grotto also has squirting water to play in. At Epcot, go to the jumping fountains outside Journey into Imagination and the pathway to World Showcase. At the Disney-MGM Studios, the leaky hose at the Honey, I Shrunk the Kids Movie Set Adventure spurts water. Nobody stays dry at Tiger Rapids Run in Disney's Animal Kingdom. There are squirting fountains at the Downtown Disney Marketplace, too.

Fort Wilderness

Fort Wilderness is tucked away in a wooded area of Walt Disney World. (It isn't really a fort. It's a campground.) You can stay overnight in trailers or just come for a day. There are tennis and volleyball courts, and a marina with lots of boats. River Country, described on page 140, is also nearby. You could spend days here and not run out of things to do. If you only have a couple of hours, explore the petting farm and rent a boat for a ride around Bay Lake.

Petting Farm

Chickens, goats, pigs, and sheep live on a small farm at Fort Wilderness. Some of the animals like people to pet them. Others enjoy eating pellets from kids' hands (you can buy their special food from a dispenser that looks like a gumball machine).

Most kids think the farm is fun. "You can get close to the animals without being afraid," says Lissy. Karyn says, "If you really like animals, you'll have fun no matter how old you are."

More Fort Wilderness Fun

Fort Wilderness offers lots of other things to do. You can rent a canoe for a trip along the campground's canals. Or you can rent a bicycle and explore one of the many trails. At the Tri-Circle-D Ranch, you can see the champion horses that pull the trolleys in the Magic Kingdom. (They live in a barn near Pioneer Hall.)

Kids over 9 years old can take a trail ride on horseback. You can also enjoy a Fort Wilderness hayride, go fishing, or rent a speedboat.

Sports

Kids who like sports can find plenty of ways to keep active at Walt Disney World. You can rent bikes or boats at one of the resorts, or play miniature golf on a course that looks like scenes from the movie *Fantasia*. To see athletes at work, visit Disney's Wide World of Sports complex. Read on to find out how.

Disney's Wide World of Sports Complex

Sports fans should plan a visit to this exciting complex. It has facilities for every sport you can imagine. The Atlanta Braves baseball team comes here for spring training. The Harlem Globetrotters basketball team trains here, too.

Watch a game

You can spend a day watching lots of amateur events. Tickets cost $6.75 for kids ages 3 through 9, and $8 for anyone 10 and older.

If you want to see a professional game, you have to buy your tickets ahead of time, and prices vary. Have a parent call 407-363-6600 for information.

Play football

Do you like to play football? If so, the NFL Experience activity area is perfect for you. There are places to practice running, passing, punting, and catching—just like the pros do! (It's on an outdoor field at the sports complex.)

> ## "It's fun because it's challenging."
>
> **Michael (age 11)**

Fantasia Gardens

If you have seen the movie *Fantasia*, you'll know how this miniature golf course got its name. Where else will you find hippos on tiptoe, dancing mushrooms, or xylophone stairs?

Every hole has a theme

The holes are grouped by musical themes. At the Dance of the Hours hole, watch the hippo standing on an alligator. If you hit the ball through the gator's mouth, the hippo dances!

A course for kids

All of the kids loved this course. Danielle T. says, "This is the best miniature golf course I've been to.

My favorite is the squirting water hole." Szasha says, "Some of the holes look really hard, but then they're not. My favorite is the blue and purple cave." "It's fun because it's challenging," Michael says. "I got a hole in one!"

Water Mouse Boats

A Water Mouse is a speedy little boat that you can rent. And it delivers big thrills. If you are 12 or older, you can drive one all by yourself.

A Water Mouse ride gets very high marks from kids. "It's awesome," says Brian L. "I was

turning into the waves and one splashed on top of me." David thinks it's neat to drive your own boat. "This is fun that you definitely can't miss," he says.

You can rent a Water Mouse boat at many Disney resorts. The cost is about $18 for a half hour.

Discovery Island

Unusual animals and endangered species have a safe home on Discovery Island. Birds of every color, miniature deer, and monkeys all live here. There are 500-pound turtles, too! It's like a natural zoo with lots of trees and plants, so it feels like a forest. There's even a hospital right on the island where injured animals are cared for. You can look in through glass windows and see the veterinarian at work.

A good place for bird-watching

The kids agree that Discovery Island is worth a visit. Most of them never even knew it existed. Lissy says, "The place is awesome."

You get to see some animals up close, like a baby alligator, a hedgehog, vultures, and gigantic turtles. "The hedgehog is pretty cute," says Ashley, "and the turtles are neat, but they smell bad."

See endangered species

David thinks Discovery Island is a "great way to see these birds, maybe for the last time. They're trying to save a lot of birds that are becoming extinct."

If you are between the ages of 7 and 15, you can sign up for a special guided tour for kids. For information about the cost and schedules, ask a parent to call 800-496-6337.

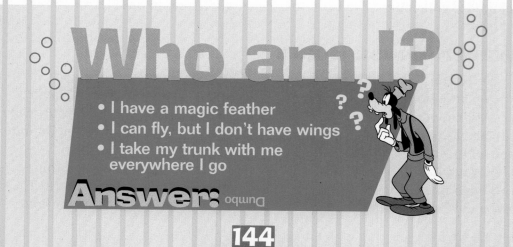

Who am I?

- I have a magic feather
- I can fly, but I don't have wings
- I take my trunk with me everywhere I go

Answer: Dumbo

Camp Disney

Disney Imagineers would make great magicians. They use tricks all the time to create special effects for attractions at Walt Disney World. Like at Voyage of The Little Mermaid when bubbles float up into the audience. It might not seem like blowing bubbles requires much magic. But it's getting them to float *up*, and not fall *down*, that's the tricky part. How do they do it? That's one of the Imagineers' best secrets. (But here's a hint: The trick wouldn't work without the help of helium.)

Can you keep a secret?

The Imagineers are very good at keeping secrets. They don't like to share the secrets behind all of the tricks they use because that could spoil the illusion. But if you're really curious, there is one place to learn some good secrets. It's called Camp Disney, at the Disney Institute.

Many of the programs at Camp Disney are about entertainment. But some are about art or nature. One of them even teaches you how to rock climb. Depending on which class you take, you might go on a behind-the-scenes tour of the Disney-MGM Studios, make your own comic strip, or go bird-watching.

So many choices

There are lots of programs to pick from, and new ones are always being added. They are popular, so be sure to plan ahead if you want to include one in your vacation. You might even be able to get school credit for some of them.

A half-day program costs $69 and a full-day program is $99. You must be at least 7 years old to participate. For more information, have a parent call 800-496-6337. The Disney Institute offers many programs for grown-ups, too— so your parents won't feel left out!

Downtown Disney

What has interesting shops and restaurants, movies, dance spots, and one of the best game centers in the world? Downtown Disney! It has three different sections: the West Side, the Marketplace, and Pleasure Island.

The West Side

This is the newest section of Downtown Disney. It has places to shop, eat, and catch a movie. It also has something called DisneyQuest. It's an incredible mix of arcade, amusement park, and virtual reality center.

At DisneyQuest you can ride Buzz Lightyear bumper cars, fight aliens in a virtual spaceship, and be a human joystick in a giant pinball game. You can also design a wild and crazy roller coaster—and then ride it in a simulator. (Warning: Don't do this with a full stomach!)

The Marketplace

Looking for that perfect souvenir? If you don't find it at the West Side, go to the Marketplace. There are dozens of shops to browse in. You can also make a wacky creation at the LEGO Imagination center. As Kirsti says, "It's the coolest! You can build things. There are also life-size Lego models, like a painter, and a dinosaur. There's even a snoring man."

Amy's favorite place to shop is the World of Disney store. It's the biggest Disney store in the world.

Pleasure Island

You might think this place is just for grown-ups—but kids can have fun at Pleasure Island. Especially kids who like to dance. Kids can bring their parents to three clubs: the brand-new Wildhorse Saloon (country music), 8TRAX (1970s tunes), and Rock 'n' Roll Beach Club (rock 'n' roll, of course).

If you don't dance, don't worry. There are also games to play, outdoor shows, and fireworks to watch every night. You can even get a temporary Mickey Mouse tattoo!

Walt Disney World Resorts

There are 19 resorts on the Walt Disney World property. That means there are enough rooms at Walt Disney World for you to stay in a different spot every night for more than 60 years!

We visited most of the resorts during our trips. To help you decide where to stay, we've provided information on some of your WDW resort choices. We paid special attention to what's most important to kids—food, arcades, and activities. All of the hotels have pools, a playground, and at least one arcade. If an arcade or playground is really cool, we mention it here. We've also included information on the best pools for kids (on the next page).

Near the Magic Kingdom

Contemporary

The monorail speeds right through the center of this hotel. There are three restaurants, seven shops, boat rentals, a large pool with a water slide, and a huge arcade. "If you love video games, you'll love this place," says Ashley P.

Fort Wilderness Resort and Campground

Bring a camper or rent a trailer home at this pretty wooded campground. There is a restaurant, boat and bike rentals, a petting farm, and pony rides.

147

Grand Floridian

At first, this elegant hotel seems to be designed for grown-ups, but it's also fun for kids. There are boats to rent, four shops, and a huge pool. The monorail stops here, too.

Polynesian

The plants and trees here make it look like a tropical island. There are shops, restaurants, boat rentals, and a monorail station. Nita and David like the pool with the slide.

Wilderness Lodge

With its log columns and totem poles, this hotel offers a taste of the American Northwest. "You really feel like you're in the wilderness," says Lindsay. Dawna likes that

"people sit in rocking chairs just watching the fire—in Florida!"

This hotel has two restaurants, a pool, bike and boat rentals, and an arcade. There are also special fishing trips just for kids.

The Best Hotel Pools for Kids

The hotel pools with water slides are the most fun for kids. Since you can only swim in the pools if you're a guest of the hotel, this will help you and your family decide where to stay. One of the best pools is Stormalong Bay at the **Yacht and Beach Club.** You can climb a wrecked ship and slide back down into the water. At **Port Orleans**, the Doubloon Lagoon pool is built around a sea serpent whose tongue is a water slide. Ol' Man Island is a recreation center at **Dixie Landings**. Its large pool has slides and ropes. At the **Polynesian**, the Swimming Pool Lagoon has a cluster of boulders that's really a water slide. The pool at the **Contemporary** has water jets and a slide. The Luna Park pool at **BoardWalk** will remind you of an amusement park, with its water-spouting elephants and Keister Coaster water slide. At **Coronado Springs**, the pool looks like a Mayan ruin. There's a pyramid and a water slide that passes under a spitting jaguar.

Near Epcot and the Disney-MGM Studios

BoardWalk

This hotel is right on a boardwalk, along with a bakery and lots of restaurants and shops. Its pool is modeled after an amusement park. Michael likes it here, especially at night. "There's entertainment, excitement, and lots to do," he says.

Caribbean Beach

The rooms at this hotel are located in many colorful buildings. There's a playground that kids really enjoy, a food court, boat and bike rentals, and one shop. "It's a pretty hotel because of all the colors," says Nita.

Dixie Landings

Many of this hotel's buildings look like old homes from the southern part of the United States. There's a restaurant and food court, pool, playground, and a fishing hole, plus boat and bike rentals.

Old Key West

The townhouses that make up this resort have all the comforts of home. The rooms have VCRs, and movie rentals are available. There are also boat and bike rentals, restaurants, and a shop.

Port Orleans

The special details at this hotel make it look like the city it's named for—New Orleans, Louisiana. There's one restaurant and a food court, a pool with a dragon slide, a playground, boat and bike rentals, and a shop.

Swan and Dolphin

You can't miss the dolphin and swan statues that sit on top of these two hotels—they're gigantic. Together the hotels have eight restaurants, an ice cream parlor, boat rentals, and five shops. You can walk to Epcot from both hotels.

The Villas at the Disney Institute

There are several types of villas, including "treehouses" on stilts. There's a restaurant, six pools, and bikes to rent. You can rent a canoe here, too. The villas are all close to Downtown Disney.

Near Animal Kingdom

All-Star Resorts

All-Star Sports has five buildings. Each one is designed around a sport—tennis, football, surfing, baseball, or basketball.

At All-Star Music the buildings are modeled around types of music—rock 'n' roll, country, calypso, Broadway show tunes, and jazz.

Each building at All-Star Movies has a movie theme, including *Toy*

Yacht and Beach Club

These are two connected hotels. There are boat rentals, restaurants, an ice cream parlor, shops, and an amazing sand-bottom pool. And the best part is you can walk to Epcot and BoardWalk from here.

Story, *The Mighty Ducks*, and *101 Dalmatians*. Each hotel has a playground, pools, and an arcade.

Coronado Springs

The land at this hotel looks like parts of the southwestern USA and Mexico. There's an arcade, boat and bike rentals, a playground, and a pool that looks like an ancient pyramid. (Look for the Hidden Mickey in a wall near the pool.)

Disney Cruise Line

Set sail on a Disney ship with Mickey and his friends. You visit Walt Disney World for a few days and then cruise to the Bahamas. The ship has special activity areas, pools, and programs just for kids, so you can do your own thing while your parents relax. Szasha says, "There's a whole deck just for kids." Dan thinks "it's not like an ordinary cruise. It's like a theme park, really." Michael agrees. "It's fun and different," he says, "and something I haven't done before." The kids think the best part is getting to explore Disney's private island called Castaway Cay. Danielle T. says, "Castaway Cay is so cool! There's all sorts of interesting things you can do. I've always wanted to go snorkeling, and I can do that there." Dan adds, "There are even water slides and scavenger hunts for kids."

Restaurants

Eating at Walt Disney World can be as much fun as riding Splash Mountain (well, almost as much fun!). Here are our suggestions for the best spots for kids to eat in each theme park and the rest of Walt Disney World.

Magic Kingdom
Best Places for Kids to Eat

Aunt Polly's Dockside Inn . . . . Peanut butter and jelly sandwiches
Casey's Corner . . . . Hot dogs
Cosmic Ray's Starlight Cafe . . . . Veggie burgers
Crystal Palace . . . . Macaroni and cheese
Fantasyland Pretzel Stand .Cinnamon pretzels
Liberty Square Market . . . . .Fruit
Lunching Pad at Rockettower Plaza . . . . Turkey legs
Main Street Bake Shop . . . . Cookies
Main Street Confectionery . . . . .Candy and krispie treats
Pecos Bill Cafe . . . . Chili
Pinocchio Village Haus . . . . Hamburgers
Plaza Ice Cream Parlor . . . . Ice cream
Plaza Pavilion . . . . Pizza
Toontown Market . . . . .Strawberry shortcake

Epcot
Best Places for Kids to Eat

Alfredo's (in Italy) . . . . Spaghetti

Cantina de San Angel (in Mexico) . . . . Nachos

Cheese and Pasta Stand (in The Land) . . . . Macaroni and cheese

Electric Umbrella (in Innoventions) . . . . Hot dogs

Kringla Bakeri og Kafe (in Norway) . . . . .Cookies

Liberty Inn (in The American Adventure) . . . . Hamburgers

Pasta Piazza Ristorante (in Innoventions) . . . . Pizza

Pure and Simple (in Wonders of Life) . . . . Fruit

Refreshment Port (near Canada) . . . . Ice cream

Sandwich Shop (in The Land) . . . . . . Peanut butter and jelly sandwiches

Sommerfest (in Germany) . . . . Soft pretzels

Süssigkeiten (in Germany) . . . . Gummi bears

Trapper Bob's Beaver Tail Cart (in Canada) . . . . .Fried dough

Disney-MGM Studios
Best Places for Kids to Eat

Animal Kingdom
Best Places for Kids to Eat

Campside Funnel Cakes . . . . Funnel cakes
Chip 'n' Dale's Cookie Cabin . . . . Cookies
Dino Diner . . . . Turkey legs
Harambe Fruit Market . . . . Fruit
Island Mercantile . . . . Candy
Mr. Kamal's Burger Grill . . . . Hamburgers
Munch Wagon . . . . Hot dogs
Pizzafari . . . . Pizza
Rainforest Cafe . . . . Veggie burgers
Restaurantosaurus . . . . Chicken nuggets and fries
Tamu Tamu Refreshments . . . . Ice cream and frozen yogurt
Tusker House . . . . Fried chicken

Eating with the Characters

Kids of all ages enjoy eating with the characters. They come right up to your table to meet you and pose for photos. As David says, "Seeing all the Disney characters joke and dance around makes the meal special."

Lots of restaurants invite the characters to their meals. They are very popular, so no matter which restaurant you choose, it's a good idea to make priority seating arrangements ahead of time. Just ask a parent to call 407-WDW-DINE (939-3463).

At the resorts

Chef Mickey serves up breakfast and dinner at Chef Mickey's restaurant in the Contemporary. Look for other characters at breakfast at 'Ohana in the Polynesian and at Garden Grove in the Swan (Saturday only). For Sunday brunch, try Harry's Safari Bar & Grille in the Dolphin.

You can eat breakfast with Mary Poppins and Alice in Wonderland at 1900 Park Fare in the Grand Floridian, or with Goofy at Cape May Cafe in the Beach Club.

Snack Wagons

All around the theme parks are wagons that sell soft drinks, popcorn, and lots of ice cream —Cookies 'n' Cream ice cream sandwiches, Mouseketeer Bars, low-fat yogurt, and strawberry bars. Some wagons offer fresh fruit and other healthy snacks.

Winnie the Pooh and his pals make appearances at Olivia's Cafe in Old Key West and at Artist Point in the Wilderness Lodge throughout the week.

Other dinner choices include 1900 Park Fare in the Grand Floridian and Gulliver's Grill at Garden Grove in the Swan (Monday, Thursday, Friday).

In the theme parks

The theme parks get in on the fun, too, with character meals throughout the day. In the Magic Kingdom, Cinderella hosts breakfast at Cinderella's Royal Table in the castle. Pooh, Tigger, and Eeyore entertain at the Crystal Palace all day long. And Goofy hosts dinner at the Liberty Tree Tavern.

In Epcot, visit Chip and Dale for any meal at the Garden Grill in The Land. Soundstage at the Disney-MGM Studios is the best place for

breakfast and lunch with characters from recent animated films. Look for familiar faces from movies such as *Aladdin*, *The Hunchback of Notre Dame*, or *Mulan*.

Captain Mickey Mouse and his crew host a character breakfast at Fulton's Crab House, between Pleasure Island and the Downtown Disney Marketplace.

HOT

Most restaurants have special menus for kids. Just ask!

TIP

Dinner Shows

Hoop-Dee-Doo Musical Review

Entertainers sing, dance, and tell jokes while you chow down on chicken, ribs, and corn. Danielle G. says, "They get everyone in on the fun and put on a wonderful show." David thinks the show is "very funny. I was laughing the whole time."

Polynesian Luau and Mickey's Tropical Review

Aloha! That means "hello" (and "goodbye") in Hawaiian. You'll hear it at both of these shows. At the luau, performers do the hula and other dances. Mickey's Tropical Revue is like a luau, but Mickey Mouse gets into the act! At both shows, waiters serve Polynesian food and fruity drinks.

All-American Backyard Barbecue

Mickey and Minnie are having a barbecue every night this summer, and you are welcome to join them. You can eat all the hot dogs and barbecued ribs you want. And for dessert, there's fresh watermelon and strawberry shortcake.

While you're eating, a live band plays country music. After dinner, there's a show for kids, games, and dancing with the Disney characters. Don't forget your cowboy hat!

> Reservations for all of these shows should be made before you arrive at Walt Disney World. Your parents can call **407-WDW-DINE (939-3463)**.

Still Hungry?

Even outside the theme parks, one thing is for sure: You'll never be far from food at Walt Disney World! Here are some great spots for kids:

Downtown Disney:
- Ghirardelli Soda Fountain and Chocolate Shop
- McDonald's
- Planet Hollywood
- Rainforest Cafe

Disney's Wide World of Sports Complex:
- Official All Star Cafe

Disney Resorts:
- Beaches & Cream Soda Shop at the Yacht and Beach Club
- Captain Cook's Snack Company at the Polynesian
- Chef Mickey's at the Contemporary
- Dolphin Fountain at the Dolphin
- 1900 Park Fare at the Grand Floridian

Magical Memories

The fun doesn't have to end when your vacation does.
Use these pages to preserve your Disney memories.

On our way to Walt Disney World, we traveled by

[ ] plane   [ ] bus   [ ] boat

[ ] car   [ ] train   [ ] flying carpet

My usual bedtime is _____ o'clock.
During the trip the latest I went to bed was _____ o'clock.
The earliest I woke up was _____ o'clock.

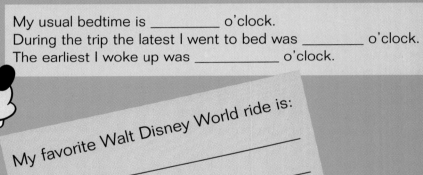

My favorite Walt Disney World ride is:
_____
_____
I like it because it is: _____

My least favorite Walt Disney World ride is:
_____

Paste your plane, train,
or bus ticket here.

My favorite thing about being on vacation was:

_____

There are so many different resorts near Walt Disney World. Here's where we stayed during our visit:

_____

I spent the most time at
[ ] Magic Kingdom
[ ] Disney-MGM Studios   [ ] Epcot
                             [ ] Disney's Animal Kingdom

Paste a Walt Disney World napkin here.

Vacations aren't just fun, they're educational, too! Here's one thing that I learned about while I was at Walt Disney World: _____

_____

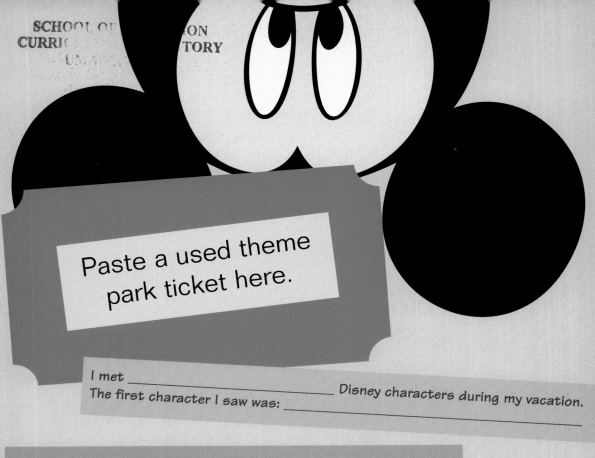

Paste a used theme
park ticket here.

I met _____ Disney characters during my vacation.
The first character I saw was: _____

My favorite restaurant was: _____
I ate: _____

The funniest thing that happened was:
_____
_____
_____

Paste a Walt Disney
World receipt here.